# Facebook Con

*Incredible devotionals.*
*What a glorious experience...*

*I'm looking forward to doing this again! Phenomenal!*

*This is exciting to read and fills me with hope.*

*I just finished my last day. What a blessing! To God be the glory!!*

*I'm looking forward to participating again in Michigan. Last year made such a change in my prayer life.*

*Already incredible!*

*I loved doing this and thinking about all the others joining in around our country. Looking forward to joining again next year.*

*Wonderful devotional. It has been a blessing. I will repeat.*

*Have SO appreciated these devotions and the challenge to pray. This is my 2$^{nd}$ year and it has been a huge blessing each time.*

*Such a great idea and so doable!*

*This will be my third year praying with you all. So blessed.*

*Praying for our nation was such a great start to the year.*

*I am amazed how quickly these 50 days have passed by. I am thankful to know we serve a mighty God who hears our prayers.*

*It has been such a blessing to be praying with so many. Thank you.*

*I have been blessed in my own walk as I prayed these 50 days!! All glory to our Almighty God!!!*

*We love the book. So profound!*

*What a total transformation this has been. The journey brought growth in the Lord. Amazing!*

*This is such a great idea and so needed. Joining from Texas.*

*It has blessed me tremendously as we bow down and ask His blessing on our nation.*

*This has been a great journey! Our prayer team at church is doing this together. Those daily writings are so good.*

*It's been a blessing completing this with our Women at War group.*

*I did this last year. Very powerful. I will participate again.*

*I am loving this study and prayer nudges! It is so strengthening to know that all the Psalms are being prayed back to the Father daily.*

*This has been one of the best studies I have participated in.*

*I can't even begin to describe what I feel today with it being the last day. This is my third year with you. It has been AMAZING!*

*This is a great program and a fantastic way to end one year and begin the new one!*

*I've been wanting to do something like this but didn't know how. Thank you for standing in the gap.*

*This is my second year going through this devotional. It has been such a blessing both times.*

*Thank you for organizing this beautiful time of intercession. It's been an honor to participate these three years.*

*My husband and I have been deeply blessed by participating again in this prayer project! What a wonderful experience!*

*Thank you for allowing me to partake in this challenge. Look forward to being a part of it again.*

*What a blessing this book has been. It is extremely well-written and biblically sound. May God use this project to transform our country.*

*One of the most purposeful actions I have seen being encouraged in a while. Count me in.*

*I am so excited to do this! Can't wait to see what our Father does.*

*Thank you so much for preparing this powerful resource! A mighty work is on the horizon.*

# If We Will...
# Then He Will

# If We Will...
# Then He Will

## A 50 State Prayer Project
## for Revival

A Three Strand Cord

SNOW
DROP
PRINT

Snowdrop Print, P. O. Box 326, Beulah, WY 82712

ISBN 979-8-9912356-0-0

*Prayer*
lays hold of
**God's plan** and
becomes the link
between **His will**
and its accomplishment

on earth.


- Elisabeth Elliot

W e thought it was just lunch. But God had something more in mind.

We are three friends from church who simply decided to get together for lunch over the Memorial Day weekend of 2021. 15 minutes into lunch, one of us said she had been asking the Lord for a couple of friends to help with an idea she believed He had given her. She shared a plan to organize prayer warriors from each State to pray for revival in America. We said "Let's do it!" The flame was lit.

We felt this was too overwhelming a job for three ordinary women from South Dakota. But if it was the Lord's will, He could make it happen. And He did, in miraculous ways! He tapped each one of our unique personalities, giftings and backgrounds to bring this to fruition. After only 7 weeks, with over 70 hours of meetings and countless hours of writing and rewriting, the original rough draft of this manuscript was complete.

We have been truly astounded and humbled at the response this project has received over the past three years. Not only are thousands of prayer warriors participating from every State in our nation, but our website has been visited by people from over 50 countries around the world. Be encouraged. The world is hungering for revival.

In response to input from past participants, this 2024 edition has been expanded to include 81 full hymn scores and lyrics. However, a free, full copy of this manuscript is available on our website for viewing, downloading or printing. Though we have copyrighted this material, we give you total freedom to reproduce it free of charge. However, you are not permitted to financially profit from its reproduction nor alter its content in any way without prior written permission. You can contact us by visiting our website: ifwewill.com or sending an email to dawn@ifwewill.com.

May Almighty God use these words to stir hearts and bring revival to this nation and around the world, for His kingdom and His glory.

A Three Strand Cord (Ecclesiastes 4:12)

# CONTENTS

# 1

# THE PURPOSE

*If My people who are called by My name will humble themselves, and pray and seek My face, and turn from their wicked ways, then I will hear from heaven, and will forgive their sin and heal their land.*                                        II Chronicles 7:14

## "If We Will...Then He Will"

If we will...then He will. What does that mean?

Many of us are feeling a growing unsettledness in our hearts. We are disturbed by the increasing immorality, division, and violence we see in our nation, and there doesn't seem to be an easy answer. We are growing fearful of the potential seismic shift in our futures.

We want our nation, our land to be healed. And that is what God promises to do, right? Yes, but it is an "If...then" proposition. "*If* we will...*then* He will." So what needs to happen *first*?

II Chronicles 7:14 tells us we *first* must humble ourselves, pray, seek His face and turn from our wicked ways. Only then will He forgive our sin and heal our land.

"If We Will...Then He Will" is a grassroots prayer project for revival that was birthed from a desire to bring repentance and renewal to the hearts of His people, those of us called by His name.

This is not motivated by politics or church affiliation. It is simply a call to His people to turn from *our* wicked ways and implore Him to heal our land. The plan prepares intercessors from all 50 states to pray for 50 days for His people and for our nation.

How? It begins on December 1 with 31 days of preparation for spiritual battle. This is followed by a time of prayer and fasting on January 1, New Year's Day. Then for 50 days - January 2 through February 20 - prayer warriors from all 50 states will be led in interceding on behalf of God's people, our nation and our world.

This is not a passive project. We have a real enemy, and we need to learn how to seriously and effectively engage in battle against him and "the spiritual forces of evil in the heavenly realms" (Ephesians 6:12 NIV). Therefore, there are 31 days of preparation for spiritual warfare, as well as a time of prayer and fasting, prior to our 50 days of intercession.

Why 50 days of prayer? The 50-day plan has specific and unique daily rotating reading assignments in Psalms for intercessors in each of the 50 states. The result is that the *entire* book of Psalms is lifted to the Lord by intercessors all across our nation *each and every day* for 50 days. Each prayer warrior will also seek the Lord daily, asking Him for the petitions He desires we bring before Him in prayer. The details are laid out on the following pages.

There is real hope for a new beginning, but only if we do it God's way. Together, this is our journey back to Him, back to our "first love" (Revelation 2:4). Only then will we be enabled to turn from our wicked ways. And only then will He heal our land.

# 2

# THE PROBLEM

*All we like sheep have gone astray; We have turned, every one, to his own way;...*                                          Isaiah 53:6a

## How Did We Get Here??

We watch in both horror and disbelief. From airplanes being used as instruments of terror on September 11, to our cities being set on fire, to sin being proudly celebrated in our streets and the exploding issues of drugs and human trafficking, we think "How did we get here??"

The answer is simple. We decided to follow our own human nature. We went astray, turning away from God and His way, His truth. We have become "lovers of self...lovers of money...lovers of pleasure rather than lovers of God" (II Timothy 3:2-4 ESV).

In the thousands of years of human history, a cycle of civilization has repeated itself over and over again. People find themselves in misery. Out of desperation, they cry out to God and experience a spiritual awakening. Delivery from misery brings liberty. Liberty, in turn, produces abundance. But sadly, abundance greatly diminishes the perception of a need for God. People begin doing what is right in their own eyes. The culture devolves into decadence as people seek more and more pleasure. And as sure as the sun rises and sets, cultures and people end up again in misery.

If we look at American history, we find a similar pattern. The great revivals of the 1700's led to great courage which bought freedom. The new nation, while not perfect, was established on Judeo-Christian values. Our founding documents reflected the founders' respect for God's moral standards. References to their dependence on Almighty God were frequent. For example, our first President, George Washington, declared "It is the duty of all nations to acknowledge the providence of Almighty God, to obey His will, to be grateful for His benefits, and humbly to implore His protection and favor." [1]

Our nation's history is filled with examples of God's protection and favor. But the resulting abundance and prosperity have predictably led to decadence. It now feels as if we are in moral freefall and headed back into misery. How sadly predictable we are.

As a nation, we have continued to turn away from God and His principles as laid out in His Word. Many believe that we have "outgrown" a belief in God, declaring we don't need God - or anyone else for that matter - telling us what to do. They claim there are no moral absolutes, no real right nor wrong. They proclaim freedom to follow their own personal moral compass, free to do whatever feels right in their own eyes.

Right in their own eyes? Where have we heard that concept before? It is repeated numerous times throughout Scripture as the Bible describes a rebellious, "stiff-necked" people turning away from God, time and time again. And predictably, it always ends up in disaster. Those who profess to be wise become fools (Romans 1:22).

So where do we go from here? Can we stop a repeat of the cycle? Yes, but only if we experience spiritual renewal. Read on to learn more about God's way to bring that about.

# 3

# THE PLAN

*If My people who are called by My name will humble themselves, and pray and seek My face, and turn from their wicked ways, then I will hear from heaven, and will forgive their sin and heal their land.*                                        II Chronicles 7:14

## What Can We Do About It?

II Chronicles 7:14 is a core verse that we will return to again and again. It is a concise description of God's prescription for the cure we desire, both for ourselves and our nation.

This remedy was given by God to Solomon following the dedication of Solomon's magnificent temple. Much like our nation, Israel had experienced an historic height of power and prosperity. So why did God choose that time to tell Solomon that His people needed to turn from their wicked ways? Because God knows human nature. He knows that, in the midst of peace and prosperity, even we, His people, can feel as though we really don't need Him, and we end up going astray, going our own way. In His love and mercy, God outlines His way for us to come back to Him.

What is God's prescription? It is pretty straightforward. It requires *our* humbling; *our* earnest prayer, seeking God with *our* whole heart, and turning from *our* wicked ways. Ouch.

We tend to think that *other* people need to stop being such sinners. Why can't *they* just turn from *their* wicked ways so we can all be blessed by God and live together in peace and harmony? Like the fairy tale, we just want to live happily ever after. We are tempted to point the finger at other people and say *their* sin is to blame. But God says it's *our* sin.

Many of us don't want to talk or even think about sin. We know the Word says "For all have sinned and fall short of the glory of God" (Romans 3:23). But we don't *really* believe that. Most of us agree we aren't perfect, but we aren't all that bad, are we? We've all made "mistakes" as we call them. But we often knew right from wrong when we chose to do wrong. Why? Because we rationalized it wasn't really all that wrong? Because we thought we could get away with it? Because everyone else did it? Or maybe just because it made us feel good?

But then the reality of our foolish and willful choices set in. The little seeds of sin, those things that felt right in our own eyes, took root in our hearts and grew until they were full blown, full grown. Then came the reaping: the broken hearts and relationships, the damaged spiritual, emotional or physical health. That wasn't part of our fairy tale. We ignored the truth that sin is pleasurable only for a season (Hebrews 11:25 KJV), but then come the consequences.

Unfortunately, there's more cold, hard truth we prefer to ignore: "Judgment must begin at the house of God" (I Peter 4:17 KJV). God's anger is particularly kindled against us, His people. Why? Because He paid the ultimate price with His life to redeem us. He opened our eyes to the truth and we experienced His grace and His goodness. And yet, in so many ways, we have chosen to turn our back on Him and go astray, go our own way. How?

Many of us as His people have lost our desire to be distinctive, to be set apart, to please Him alone. We find ourselves more focused on personal happiness and less on personal holiness. We may be choosing the comfort of lukewarm so we can straddle that fence – just enough repentance to get to heaven but just enough sin to feel good here. Many of us who call ourselves Christians are either secretly or openly in addiction to the pleasures of food, alcohol, pornography or other sexual immoralities. There now is very little difference in the moral metrics between "Christians" and the world. Is it because we have deposed God Almighty and elevated our pleasures to reign on the throne of our lives? Is that why our culture suddenly feels like a run-away train? Are *our* compromises to blame?

Some of us have bought and repeat the lie that people don't need to turn from their sin because "God will understand." Some even go so far as to teach that what we used to call sin isn't even sin anymore. In an attempt to embrace the sinner, some of us have ended up endorsing the sin. And some have even joined in rebuking and mocking those who remain true to God's Word.

Jesus joins the world in calling us hypocrites; we may honor Him with our mouths, but our hearts are far from Him; we worship Him in vain and our teachings are just human rules (Matthew 15:7-9 NIV). No wonder we fear judgment is just around the corner. Because it is.

What can we do about it? God has a remedy. He is bringing us to a recognition of our need for spiritual re-awakening. That may be why you are reading this right now. You may be sensing a desperation, a fear that our world of comfort and ease is quickly falling away. This fear helps turn us from the foolishness of our ways and return to the wisdom of His ways.

"If We Will…Then He Will" helps us "turn" and "return" together:

**Part I** consists of 31 days of preparation. Why? Because we are preparing for battle. Part I begins December 1 and ends on New Year's Eve. Each day, we will read and meditate on a different chapter of Proverbs. Why Proverbs? Because two of the greatest deficiencies in our nation are wisdom and the distinction between right and wrong. We need training and reinforcement in both areas before we head into battle.

We also will be looking at several verses for instruction, including II Chronicles 7:14 and James 5:16, and topics such as the armor of God. The purpose of this preparation is to make us more fit and effective prayer warriors for our 50 days of intercession to follow.

**Part II** of this program is a time of prayer and fasting on New Year's Day, January 1. This day immediately precedes the 50 days of intercession. What this time of prayer and fasting will look like for you is just between you and the Lord. No one else needs to know what you are doing; but the Lord will know and promises to hear (Matthew 6:18 NIV).

**Part III** consists of 50 days of intercession, starting on January 2 and ending on February 20. We will be reading the book of Psalms together as a catalyst to remind us of God's greatness, of our neediness, and of His faithfulness to answer those who cry out to Him in repentance and desperate dependence. Each daily rotating reading in Psalms will then be followed by our praises and petitions as He leads us in intercession each day.

As each rotating division in Psalms is lifted to the Lord each day from each State, the *entire* book of Psalms will be read to the Lord *each and every day* for 50 days. Additionally, by the end of the 50 days, each prayer warrior will have read the entire book of Psalms.

We can expect Him not only to hear, but also to answer our prayers. Why? Because He says so. But there also are many amazing stories in our nation's history of when He has miraculously answered our prayers. The detailed story of General Patton's prayer is just one of many such examples scattered throughout the pages of our history as a nation. May you be encouraged as you read the following historical account.

# 4

# THE POWER

*My help comes from the LORD, who made heaven and earth.*
                                                    Psalm 121:2

## The Power of Prayer

Have there been times in history when people have cried out to God Almighty and He has answered in miraculous ways? Absolutely!

One of the most recent and well-documented events in American and world history happened in December of 1944 during World War II's pivotal Battle of the Bulge.

General Patton wrote in his journal "Know of nothing more I can do to prepare for this attack except to read the Bible and pray." [2] But after seeking the Lord's face, he must have been led to do more. Patton contacted the Army's Chief Chaplain, James H. O'Neill, and organized a call for all the troops to pray. The result? Six days of uncharacteristically clear weather for Europe in December, the dead of winter. Those six days of clear skies turned the tide of World War II.

Here are the fascinating details:

From September to December, fog and rain had plagued General Patton and his soldiers, limiting their use of air power. On the morning of December 8, 1944, Patton called the Army's Chief Chaplain, James H. O'Neill. "This is General Patton; do you have a good prayer for weather? We must do something about those rains if we are to win the war." [3]

General Patton told the Chief Chaplain "I am a strong believer in prayer. Up to now, in the Third Army, God has been very good to us. This is because a lot of people back home are praying for us. But we have to pray for ourselves, too. We've got to get not only the chaplains but every man in the Third Army to pray. We must ask God to stop these rains. If we all pray, it will be like plugging in on a current whose source is in Heaven. It is power." [4]

Within the hour, a prayer had been written and approved. Patton ordered 250,000 prayer cards produced, and then distributed to each soldier in the Third Army. With the presses working day and night, both the printing and distribution were accomplished by December 14, only six days after the order had been given. Each soldier had a prayer card in hand as they anxiously awaited the next battle. They did not have long to wait.

Just two days later, on December 16, 1944, German forces launched a surprise offensive, aided by the cover of "heavy rains, thick fogs and swirling ground mists that muffled sound, blotted out the sun, and reduced visibility to a few yards," wrote the Chief Chaplain. "For three days it looked to the jubilant Nazis as if their desperate gamble would succeed." [5]

But then the anguished and totally dependent prayers of the Allied soldiers facing defeat were answered with a miracle. The Chief Chaplain continues his eyewitness account:

"On December 20, to the consternation of the Germans and the delight of the American forecasters who were equally surprised at the turn-about, the rains and the fogs ceased. For the better part of a week came bright clear skies and perfect flying weather. General Patton prayed for fair weather for battle. He got it." [6]

Prayer turned the tide. This was the prayer on that card: [7]

## PRAYER

Almighty and most merciful Father, we humbly beseech Thee, of Thy great goodness, to restrain these immoderate rains with which we have had to contend. Grant us fair weather for Battle. Graciously hearken to us as soldiers who call upon Thee that armed with Thy power, we may advance from victory to victory, and crush the oppression and wickedness of our enemies, and establish Thy justice among men and nations. Amen.

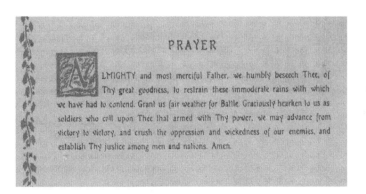

What made this prayer so miraculously powerful? It certainly wasn't the size of the card; it was no larger than a business card. It certainly wasn't the quantity of words; it could be read aloud in 30 seconds or less. It was the condition of the heart of the "pray-er" and the powerful God they were praying to.

This prayer would have been prayed whole-heartedly, fervently. Imagine if we were in the trenches. It was a time of desperation, of total dependence. God was their *only* hope, their *only* salvation. And Almighty God delivered in a remarkable way.

The Nazis' attack on December 16 was a surprise to the Allied Forces. But it was not a surprise to Almighty God. God had already pre-arranged for the Third Army soldiers to have the prayer cards in hand by December 14th, two days *prior* to the surprise attack.

The Nazis' goal was to strike fear in the hearts of the Third Army. The Nazis' surprise attack and three days of victory under cover of cloud and fog surely would have struck fear in their hearts. But that fear is precisely what God used to bring those same soldiers to the point of total desperation, of total dependence, of turning to Him in prayer because they recognized they had nowhere else to turn. "When I am afraid, I will put my trust and faith in You" (Psalm 56:3 AMP).

General Patton and the Third Army found themselves in circumstances that may not feel all that much different from our circumstances today. It may seem to us as though we are surrounded by difficulties on all sides, leaving us feeling helpless and hopeless in our own strength. And that is precisely where He wants us. Only then will we truly seek Him with our whole heart. And He promises that then we will surely find Him (Jeremiah 29:13).

May this story fortify us with courage as we prepare to engage in spiritual warfare to turn the hearts of His people and our nation back to Him.

# 5

# THE PREPARATION

*If My people who are called by My name will humble themselves, and pray and seek My face, and turn from their wicked ways, then I will hear from heaven, and will forgive their sin and heal their land.*
II Chronicles 7:14

## 31 Days of Preparation

Before engaging in battle, warriors are wise to go through some basic training. We need to understand our purpose, our goal. We need to become familiar with our defensive armor and our offensive weapons. We need to know our enemy. But it is even more important to know our Commander who leads us in battle. Hence these 31 Days of Preparation.

On the following pages, you will find 31 daily assignments. We will be reading through the entire book of Proverbs together, one chapter each day. We also will be dissecting a few verses and topics such as fervent prayer and the armor of God to prepare us for battle.

You may want to grab a journal to write a personal application at the end of each day's devotion. Taking time to put something in writing helps us cement that day's truth in our hearts and minds, and remind us of what we have learned.

You will find a hymn included opposite each daily devotion. Having these familiar hymns running in the background of our minds can help keep us focused on Him and our mission as we navigate the busyness of each day. We would encourage you to sing at least one verse of these hymns, even if only mentally. It will help bring its message of truth and encouragement to your mind throughout the day. If the hymn is not familiar, there are multiple renditions online that can facilitate their deep ministry to our souls.

Our daily assignment will also include a time to come before our Heavenly Father in prayer with an open heart. Together, we will ask Him to closely examine our hearts, to show us if we are harboring any willful ways and enable us to turn from them. Why? Because we want to be effective warriors in His army. We want to push back the enemy on every front. We want to take back every bit of territory that has been surrendered to the enemy, and then some!

But why are we still focused on II Chronicles 7:14? Because repentance and renewal are both integral and often overlooked ingredients in God's prescription. In fact, this Scripture is so important to our training, we will be spending the first nine days of preparation looking at various aspects of this instructional verse.

Some of us are coming to this project with the idea of just lifting up America, asking God to heal our land. But in these 31 days of preparation, we will see that the healing of our land is only a byproduct. The root problem is not *those* wicked people who won't stop sinning. The root problem lies with *us* if our hearts are not fervently, whole-heartedly seeking after God.

Let's allow the Lord to examine our hearts. Let's turn from our lukewarm love and our wayward ways. Let's return to the passion of our first love with Him. Let's learn how to "put on the whole armor of God" (Ephesians 6:11) and wield our powerful weapons, which are "mighty through God to the pulling down of strongholds" (II Corinthians 10:4 KJV).

If our Lord has laid it on your heart to intercede for spiritual revival in our nation, we invite you to join us in this project. If you want to be counted as a prayer warrior for our country, now is the time. This is the place. Basic training starts on the following page on December 1.

Let the preparation begin.

*The horse is made ready for the day of battle, but victory rests with the Lord.*                                      Proverbs 21:31(NIV)

# Amazing Grace!

# December 1                                    Called

*If My people who are called by My name...* II Chronicles 7:14

It may seem obvious, but this is a call to action only for His people. We need to be His, called by His name. What does that mean?

Unfortunately, it doesn't mean if *we* call ourselves Christians. It means if *He* calls us His. Is He our Savior, our Redeemer? Have we accepted His free gift of salvation purchased for us by Jesus?

Let's get real with Him. We can't pretend or hide anything from God Almighty. If we have accepted Jesus as our Savior, has our profession of faith become little more than lip service?

Let's examine our hearts, and see if we aren't counting our "pew warming" or other good deeds to earn us a spot on the team. Have we ever truly come to the end of our "selves" and given up our seat on the throne of our lives? Are we totally committed to His truth, His ways, His plan? Does our faith truly guide our thoughts and actions? Or are we hanging out in the limbo of lukewarm?

Now is the time to get off the fence. Now is the time to truly get right with God Almighty, our Creator, our Redeemer, our Shepherd and Friend.

Let's together take a moment to confirm with Him that He is firmly seated on the throne of our lives and that we are committed to following Him, no matter what. If we have drifted into lukewarm, let's ask Him to make us firmly grounded in His truth and set us on fire for Him.

**Today's Action:** Let's read the complete chapter of Proverbs 1 together today, asking Him to let His truth and wisdom sink into our renewed and refreshed hearts. We do not want to be that fool who despises wisdom and instruction.

*The fear of the LORD is the beginning of knowledge, but fools despise wisdom and instruction.*     Proverbs 1:7

# Have Thine Own Way, Lord

1. Have Thine own way, Lord! Have Thine own way!___ Thou art the pot - ter, I am the clay!___ Mold me and make me Af - ter Thy will,___ While I am wait - ing, Yiel-ded and still.

2. Have Thine own way, Lord! Have Thy own way!___ Search me and try me, Mas - ter, to - day!___ Whi - ter than snow, Lord, Wash me just now,___ As in Thy pre - sence Hum-bly I bow.

3. Have Thine own way, Lord! Have Thine own way!___ Woun-ded and wea - ry, Help me, I pray!___ Po - wer, all po - wer Sure - ly is Thine!___ Touch me and heal me, Sa - vior di - vine.

4. Have Thine own way, Lord! Have Thine own way!___ Hold o'er my be - ing Ab - so - lute sway!___ Fill with Thy Spi - rit Till all shall see___ Christ on - ly, al - ways, Li - ving in me.

*Hymnary.org*

# December 2                                    Teachable

*...will humble themselves...* II Chronicles 7:14

After confirming that we are His, the next thing God tells us to do is to humble ourselves. Why?

Think of the most prideful person you know. They usually are arrogant. They know it all. They have all the answers. And if they don't have an answer, they are sure they are smart enough to figure it out on their own. They certainly don't need anyone else to tell them how to live their lives. They are not teachable.

What does God say about a prideful person like this? He says that person is a fool (Proverbs 12:15). Why? Because God's ways are higher than our ways (Isaiah 55:9); therefore, our ways are foolishness to Him. His ways are the best ways; they are the right ways; His ways will ultimately bring us the most fulfillment.

God's ways may not seem or feel right to us because of our limited understanding. That is why we need to humble ourselves. We need to admit we don't know it all. We need to admit that He is God and we are not. We need to allow ourselves to be taught His ways. And we only can be taught when we are humbly teachable.

Let's come in humility before our Almighty and all-wise, all-knowing God, admitting that He is God and we are not, that His ways are better than our ways. Then, let's ask Him to lead us in His higher ways.

**Today's Action**: Together, let's read every word of the 2nd chapter of Proverbs, asking Him to empty our hearts and minds of pride in our own ways, so that we will have plenty of room to soak up His wisdom and His ways.

*Indeed, if you call out for insight and cry aloud for*
*understanding, and if you look for it as for silver and*
*search for it as for hidden treasure, then you will understand*
*the fear of the LORD and find the knowledge of God.*
Proverbs 2:3-5 NIV

# Trust and Obey

1. When we walk with the Lord In the light of His Word
2. Not a bur-den we bear, Not a sor-row we share,
3. But we ne-ver can prove The de-lights of his love
4. Then in fel-low-ship sweet We will sit at His feet

What a glo-ry He sheds on our way! Let us do His good will;
But our toil He doth rich-ly re-pay; Not a grief or a loss,
Un-til all on the al-tar we lay; For the fa-vor He shows
Or we'll walk by His side in the way; What he says we will do,

He a-bides with us still, And with all who will trust and o-bey.
Not a frown or a cross, But is blest if we trust and o-bey.
And the joy He be-stows Are for them who will trust and o-bey.
Where He sends we will go; Ne-ver fear, on-ly trust and o-bey.

Trust and o-bey, for there's no o-ther way To be

hap-py in Je-sus, But to trust and o-bey.

Text: John H. Sammis, 1846-1919
Tune: Daniel B. Towner, 1850-1919

Irregular
TRUST AND OBEY
www.hymnary.org/text/when_we_walk_with_the_lord

# December 3                                     His Child

*...and pray...* II Chronicles 7:14

After we have confirmed that we are His people and have humbled ourselves before Him, God instructs us to pray. Why?

Immersing ourselves in Proverbs, our faith can feel like nothing more than a long list of *do's* and *don'ts*, mostly *don'ts*. But our Heavenly Father, through Jesus, welcomes us as His children into *relationship*, not religiosity. A vital father-child relationship requires open, two-way communication. He invites us to be in moment-by-moment relationship with Him. That's prayer.

Prayer is simply talking things over with God, much like when we call up a friend and share what's on our heart and mind. We can bring all our concerns to Him, asking for His advice and counsel. (By the way, after taking time to listen, we are wise to follow His advice.)

We can't just dial God up on the phone, so how exactly do we do it? Just start talking. Share our hearts with Him. He already knows what's there. But talking about it helps *us* know what's there.

It's best to start our talk by praising Him for who He is and what He has done. That makes it easier for us to settle our hearts, to be still and know that He is God (Psalm 46:10). Then it is easier to choose to trust Him with our whole heart and not rely on our own understanding (Proverbs 3:5).

Let's humbly come and bow before His Throne, bringing our praises and petitions to Him, recognizing that He alone is God. Let's share our hearts openly with Him so His truth can bring light and life to their every little corner. Then we will be free to simply trust and obey.

**Today's Action**: Let's read each word of Proverbs 3 together, letting the Lord show us where we may be deceived into seeing ourselves as *wise in our own eyes.*

*Do not be wise in your own eyes; fear the LORD and depart from evil.*
*It will bring health to your flesh, and strength to your bones.*
Proverbs 3:7-8

# Turn Your Eyes upon Jesus

Helen Howarth Lemmel, 1922

1. O soul, are you wear-y and trou - bled? No light in the dark-ness you
2. Through death in - to life ev - er - last - ing He passed, and we fol - low Him
3. His Word shall not fail you— He prom - ised; Be - lieve Him, and all will be

see? There's a light for a look at the Sav - ior, And life more a - bun - dant and
there; Ov - er us sin no more hath do - min - ion— For more than con - quer-ors we
well: Th - en go to a world that is dy - ing, His per - fect sal - va - tion to

**Refrain**

free!
are! Turn your eyes up-on Je - sus, Look full in His won-der-ful face, And the
tell!

things of earth will grow strange-ly dim, In the light of His glo-ry and grace.

# December 4                                          Seeking Him

*...and seek My face...*II Chronicles 7:14

After humbling ourselves and praying, the Lord instructs us to seek His face. He just told us to pray; now He says to seek His face. Isn't that the same thing? Yes…and no.

Prayer often ends up being a one-way conversation, where we do all the talking. Most often, we don't even stop to listen to what is on His heart, let alone follow through.

Seeking implies searching, earnestly, with a whole heart. If it is half-hearted, it is not truly seeking. Seeking "His face" implies we are looking to visit with Him personally, to see Him face-to-face and have a one-on-one conversation. And by His amazing plan of prayer, we get to enjoy that intimate communication at any time we are willing to take the time.

Part of the purpose of dialogue is to understand one another and get on the same page. But let's be honest here. Are we truly seeking God to understand His heart? Do we truly desire to align our lives in agreement with His plans? Or are we just trying to get Him on board with ours?

If we find our prayers being half-hearted, the problem may be that we are not open to the input of our *other half,* our unconditionally loving Heavenly Father. Let's earnestly, with a whole heart, seek His face. Let's listen for His voice, His leading, and then act on how He directs.

Remember His promise that if we seek Him with our whole heart, we will surely find Him, and He will bring us back from our captivity (Jeremiah 29:13-14).

**Today's Action**: Let's read Proverbs 4 together, not half-heartedly, but with a whole heart, paying attention and listening closely to His wisdom and instruction for us.

*My son, give attention to my words; incline your ear to my sayings. Do not let them depart from your eyes; keep them in the midst of your heart; for they are life to those who find them, and health to all their flesh.*
Proverbs 4:20-22

# Whiter than Snow

1. Lord Je - sus, I long to be per - fect - ly whole;
2. Lord Je - sus, look down from Thy throne in the skies.
3. Lord Je - sus, for this I most humb - ly en - treat;
4. Lord Je - sus, Thou se - est I pa - tient - ly wait;

I want Thee for - ev - er to live in my soul;
And help me to make a com - plete sac - ri - fice;
I wait, bless - ed Lord, at Thy cru - ci - fied feet,
Come now, and with - in me a new heart cre - ate;

Break down ev - 'ry i - dol, cast out ev - 'ry foe:
I give up my - self and what - ev - er I know;
By faith, for my cleans - ing, I see Thy blood flow—
To those who have sought Thee, Thou nev - er saidst "No:"

*Chorus*

Now wash me, and I shall be whit - er than snow. Whit - er than snow,

yes, whit - er than snow; Now wash me, and I shall be whit - er than snow.

Words: James Nicholson
Music: William G. Fischer

# December 5 Set Free

*...and turn from their wicked ways...* II Chronicles 7:14

Why does God instruct us, His people, to first humble ourselves, *then* pray, *then* earnestly seek His face before directing us to turn from our wicked ways? Is it possibly because, without humbling ourselves and praying and earnestly seeking His face, that we, His people who know better, have more difficulty turning from our wicked ways?

Sometimes we who call ourselves Christians can be experts at fooling ourselves. We can have such whitewashed outsides and such filthy insides. And sometimes we are so deceived that we can't even see our own wickedness...or are *unwilling* to see it.

We tend to think that God's judgment is a result of the wickedness of others – those ungodly, sinful people of the world – not us. But this instruction is to *us*. It's *our* wickedness bringing His judgment. Unless we, His people, turn from *our* wicked ways, He will not heal our land.

Have we ever truly repented of our sins, asked for and received forgiveness, and forsaken those sins? We need to ask God Himself, who already knows *all* things, to search our hearts, show us our wicked ways, and enable us to turn from them.

Let's ask God to reveal to us any unbelief, pride or flat-out disobedience that we may not even see lurking in the shadows of our heart and mind. Let's also ask Him to shine His light on any "little" "secret" sins we are trying to hide, so He can enable us to walk away in freedom, once and for all.

**Today's Action:** Let's read Proverbs 5 together, asking the Lord to help us welcome His discipline and rejoice in His correction, because it alone can keep us from great destruction.

> *For your ways are in full view of the LORD, and He exam-*
> *ines all your paths. The evil deeds of the wicked ensnare*
> *them; the cords of their sins hold them fast. For lack of*
> *discipline they will die, led astray by their own great folly.*
> Proverbs 5:21-23 **NIV**

# Just As I Am

1. Just___ as I am,___ with-out one plea, But that___ Thy
2. Just___ as I am,___ and wait-ing not To rid___ my
3. Just___ as I am,___ tho' tossed a-bout With man-y a
4. Just___ as I am,___ poor, wretch-ed, blind; Sight, rich - es,
5. Just___ as I am,___ Thou wilt___ re-ceive, Wilt wel - come,
6. Just___ as I am,___ Thy love___ un-known Hath bro - ken

blood was shed for me, And___ that Thou bidd'st___ me
soul of one dark blot, To___ Thee whose blood___ can
con - flict, many a doubt, Figh - tings with - in___ and
heal - ing of the mind, Yea, all I need___ in
par - don, cleanse, re - lieve, Be - cause Thy pro - mise
ev' - ry bar - rier down; Now to be Thine,___ yea,

come to Thee, O Lamb of God,___ I come! I come!
cleanse each spot, O Lamb of God,___ I come! I come!
fears with - out, O Lamb of God,___ I come! I come!
Thee to find, O Lamb of God,___ I come! I come!
I be - lieve, O Lamb of God,___ I come! I come!
Thine a - lone, O Lamb of God,___ I come! I come!

Text: Charlotte Elliott, 1789-1871
Tune: William B. Bradbury, 1816-1868

88 88
WOODWORTH
www.hymnary.org/text/just_as_i_am_without_one_plea

# December 6                  Then

*...then...* II Chronicles 7:14

Then? Yes, just *then*. We are camping out on just this one word today in our 31 days of preparation for battle because it is such a pivotal word.

II Chronicles 7:14 is an "If, then" proposition. If we will, then He will. But the opposite is also true. If we will not, then He will not. If we, His people, will not humble ourselves, pray, seek His face, and turn from our wicked ways, then He will not heal our land.

Do not be deceived. God will not be mocked. He says we will reap what we sow (Galatians 6:7). Just one honest look at our country clearly shows that we, His people, have sown poorly. *We* are called to turn from *our* wicked ways. We truly believe it is His plan to heal our land. But if some of us refuse to turn, God may expose us for the whitewashed-outside, filthy-inside hypocrites we are.

Judgment starts with us, the household of God (I Peter 4:17). This is serious business. Let's voluntarily choose to come to repentance now and avoid the public scandal and tarnishing of His name (as if our current waywardness or wickedness is not already tarnishing His name). What fools we "wise-in-our-own-eyes" hypocrites can be!

Let's humbly come before our Great Physician and submit our hearts to open heart surgery. Let's allow Him to examine every chamber, shining His light of truth into every little nook and cranny, so we can be fully restored and healed. Only then will He heal our land.

**Today's Action:** Let's read Proverbs 6 together, allowing the light of His teachings and the correction of His instruction guide us in the way of life.

> *For the commandment is a lamp, and the law a light;*
> *reproofs of instruction are the way of life. Can a man*
> *take fire to his bosom, and his clothes not be burned?*
> *Can one walk on hot coals, and his feet not be seared?*
> Proverbs 6:23; 27-28

# Breathe on Me, Breath of God

1. Breathe on me, Breath of God, Fill me with life a - new,
2. Breathe on me, Breath of God, Un - til my heart is pure,
3. Breathe on me, Breath of God, Till I am whol - ly Thine,
4. Breathe on me, Breath of God, so shall I ne - ver die,

That I may love what Thou dost
Un - til with Thee I will Thy
Till all this earth - ly part of
But live with Thee the per - fect

love, And do____ what Thou wouldst do.
will, To do____ and to en - dure.
me glows with____ Thy fire di - vine.
life Of Thine____ e - ter - ni - ty.

Hymnary.org

# December 7            Wholly His

*...I will hear from heaven...*II Chronicles 7:14

After we humble ourselves, pray, seek His face, *and* turn from our wicked ways, the Lord of Hosts says He will hear from heaven. What does He hear? Psalm 102:19-20 (AMP) tells us that He looks down from the holy height of His sanctuary of heaven and searches the earth in order to hear the prisoner's sigh. A simple sigh. He listens for our sighs, our dependent cries, in order to set us free. How amazing is our God!

Yet, while we stand amazed that He searches out even a sigh, we somehow think He doesn't really see what we don't want Him to see. How ludicrous to think we can get away with the "secret" sins we harbor in the recesses of our hearts.

Proverbs is packed with warning about falling prey to sin, particularly sexual sin. Why such a focus? Is it because it often begins almost imperceptibly and then suddenly is in full bloom? Or because we think it's just "our little secret" that no one else knows about? Fools are we, thinking we can fool God!

"Choose you this day whom you will serve" (Joshua 24:15). Will you choose to turn to God and truly give up your "hidden" sin? Or will you choose to turn away because, like Gollum in Tolkien's *Lord of the Rings*, you are unwilling to give up *My Precious,* your "secret" sin?

Let's humbly come before our all-knowing God and King, asking Him to again search our hearts. If we have not already done so, let's ask Him to help us to, once and for all, let go of our "little" "secret" sins.

**Today's Action:** Let's read Chapter 7 of Proverbs together, choosing to apply His direct, but loving, words of warning to our hearts so that we might not sin against Him.

> *With much seductive speech she persuades him; with her
> smooth talk she compels him. All at once he follows her,
> as an ox goes to the slaughter, or as a stag is caught fast 'til
> an arrow pierces its liver; as a bird rushes into a snare; he does
> not know that it will cost him his life.*    Proverbs 7:21-23 ESV

# He Lifted Me

1. In lov-ing-kind-ness Je-sus came My soul in mer-cy to re-claim,
2. He called me long be-fore I heard, Be-fore my sin-ful heart was stirred,
3. His brow was pierced with many a thorn, His hands by cru-el nails were torn,
4. Now on a high-er plane I dwell, And with my soul I know 'tis well;

And from the depths of sin and shame Thru grace He lift-ed me.
But when I took Him at His word, For-giv'n He lift-ed me.
When from my guilt and grief for-lorn, In love He lift-ed me.
Yet how or why, I can-not tell. He should have lift-ed me.

He lift-ed me.

**Chorus**

From sink-ing sand, He lift-ed me, With ten-der hand, He lift-ed me,

From shades of night to planes of light, O praise His name, He lift-ed me!

Words by Charlotte G. Homer
Words by Charles H. Gabriel

PDHymns.com

# December 8                                        Forgiven

*...and will forgive their sin...*II Chronicles 7:14

We are into the 8th day of preparation and we still haven't gotten to the "heal our land" part. Why does God first say that He will forgive our sins before He says that He will heal our land?

To reinforce the truth. The truth is that we need to turn from our wicked ways and receive forgiveness before He will heal our land.

We probably want our land healed so we don't have to experience discomfort. We don't like being mocked for our faith, nor the idea of being persecuted for our convictions. We fear that the persecution of believers around the globe may be headed to our shores. We just want our comfortable life back, with its blissful ignorance or tolerance of sin.

But God is deadly serious about sin, even if we are not. Why else would He come down to earth to live a perfect life and die such an unimaginably painful, excruciating death if sin wasn't such a matter of life and death for all eternity?

We are seeking a happier life; but God is after a *holier* life. Let's double down on our commitment to choose a holier life, in line with His Word. Only then can we experience a truly joyful, fulfilled life.

Let's humbly approach the Throne of Grace today, rejoicing in His grace that offers us forgiveness of our sin through the substitutionary death of Jesus on the cross. Let's revel in the fact that "as far as the east is from the west," that is how far He has removed our sins from us (Psalm 103:12). Having been saved from the eternal penalty of our sin, let us now seek to know and do His will.

**Today's Action:** Together let's read Proverbs 8, choosing to value His words of wisdom and instruction over anything else in this world, letting them penctrate and change our willful hearts.

*Receive my instruction and not silver, and knowledge*
*rather than choice gold; for wisdom is better than rubies,*
*and all the things one may desire cannot be compared with her.*
Proverbs 8:10-11

# Channels Only

1. How I praise Thee, pre - cious Sav - ior, That Thy love laid hold of me;
2. Just a chan - nel, full of bless - ing, To the thirst - y hearts a - round,
3. Emp - tied that Thou should - est fill me, A clean ves - sel in Thine hand;
4. Wit - ness - ing Thy pow'r to save me, Set - ting free from self and sin;
5. Je - sus, fill now with Thy Spir - it Hearts that full sur - ren - der know,

Thou hast saved and cleansed and filled me, That I might Thy chan - nel be.
To tell out Thy full sal - va - tion, All Thy lov - ing mes - sage sound.
With no pow'r but as Thou giv - est Gra - cious - ly with each com - mand.
Thou who bought me to pos - sess me, In Thy full - ness, Lord, come in.
That the streams of liv - ing wa - ter From our in - ner man may flow.

**Chorus**

Chan - nels on - ly, bless - ed Mas - ter, But with all Thy won - drous pow'r

Flow - ing thru us Thou canst use us Ev - 'ry day and ev - 'ry hour.

Words: Mary E. Maxwell
Music: Ada Rose

# December 9                            Renewal

*...and heal their land.* II Chronicles 7:14

Well, finally, we are getting to the point that we thought we were looking for in the first place – healing our land! We tend to think healing our land is the end game. We do want our land healed, but what does that look like? Is it a return to *normal,* a return to *the good life,* not having to worry about our bank accounts shrinking, our comforts or our security threatened? If so, we are focused on the *stuff,* not the *substance* of life.

We must not expect that if God heals our land, life will go back to the way we were. Why? Because the way we were was not God-honoring. We were lost in lukewarm, acting blissfully ignorant, or complacently tolerant, of sin. Why would God answer our fervent prayers by returning us to *that* state? That is what got us in trouble in the first place. He has much more in mind. Revival. Repentance. Renewal.

The most essential and life-changing result of our intercession would be the cleansing and healing of our hearts. The healing of our land is only a side benefit, a symptom and sign of a healing of His people.

Imagine revival! Imagine how our world could change if His truth controlled our hearts and minds. Walking in integrity, our compassionate hearts would focus our energies and resources to be the hands and feet of Jesus worldwide. We would stand up for persecuted Christians, both here and abroad. We would be filled with an urgency to spread the Good News, to fulfill the Great Commission. We would see not only a healing of our land, but a healing of our world.

Let's praise the Lord for the opportunity to turn from our wicked ways and receive forgiveness; let's ask Him to heal our hearts so we can be used by Him to bring healing to our land and our world.

**Today's Action:** Let's read Proverbs 9 together, taking the time to let its wisdom and correction change our hearts and our lives, so we can live a long and fruitful life for Him and His purposes.

> *For by me your days will be multiplied,*
> *and years of life will be added to you.*
> Proverbs 9:11

# Teach Me Thy Way O Lord

1. Teach me Thy way, O Lord, teach me Thy way! Thy guid-ing
2. When I am sad at heart, teach me Thy way! When earth-ly
3. When doubts and fears a-rise, teach me Thy way! When storm clouds
4. Long as my life shall last, teach me Thy way! Wher-e'er my

grace af-ford teach me Thy way! Help me to walk a-right,
joys de-part, teach me Thy way! In hours of lone-li-ness,
fill the skies, teach me Thy way! Shine thru the wind and rain,
lot be cast, teach me Thy way! Un-til the race is run,

more by faith, less by sight; Lead me with heav'n-ly light, teach me Thy way!
in times of dire dis-tress, In fail-ure or suc-cess, teach me Thy way!
thru sor-row, grief and pain; Make now my path-way plain, teach me Thy way!
un-til the jour-ney's done, Un-til the crown is won, teach me Thy way!

Words and Music: B. Mansell Ramsey

# December 10                                    Fervent

*The effective, fervent prayer of a righteous man avails much.*
James 5:16b

As we prepare for battle, we certainly would want to know how to pray prayers that are effective, that "avail much". This verse indicates that our prayers need to be fervent. But what does it mean to pray fervently?

The word "fervent" has been defined as "passionate; heartfelt; wholehearted". Those descriptions help us realize that fervent prayer is not a matter of the words, the style or the length. It's a matter of the heart, a whole heart. The many words of a "babbling fool" are powerless since their goal is to impress, not to implore with a whole heart.

"Fervent" is the opposite of "half-hearted." A half-hearted prayer, even of a righteous one, will not avail much. We need to believe with all our hearts that He alone has the power to convict; He alone has the power to save; He alone has the power to restore.

James doesn't give us any more detail defining or describing fervent prayer. There isn't a to-do list like "Set your alarm to go off every hour and then pray, totally focused, for five minutes every hour for ten days." Wouldn't we like a description like that? Then we could feel like we had met the mark. We had achieved. We had accomplished. Given a specific 5-step program, we would do the five steps and then be proud of *our* accomplishment. We would lose sight of our need for a moment-by-moment dependence on Him. We need Him every moment to guide us in our prayers so we stay in line with His will and His kingdom purposes.

Let's wholeheartedly seek His face so we can be on the same page as our Commander, seeking His will and accepting His commandments so we can be more effective and fervent prayer warriors in this battle.

**Today's Action:** Let's read Proverbs 10 together, asking Him to direct us in the way of the wise, keeping us from the way of the wicked and the folly of the fool.

*The wise of heart will receive commandments, but*
*a babbling fool will come to ruin.* Proverbs 10:8 ESV

# Nothing but the Blood

1. What can wash a - way my sin? Noth-ing but the blood of
2. For my par - don this I see: noth-ing but the blood of
3. Noth - ing can for sin a - tone: noth-ing but the blood of
4. This is all my hope and peace: noth-ing but the blood of

Je - sus. What can make me whole a - gain?
Je - sus. For my clean - sing this my plea:
Je - sus. Naught of good that I have done:
Je - sus. This is all my right -eous - ness:

Noth-ing but the blood of Je - sus.
noth-ing but the blood of Je - sus.
noth-ing but the blood of Je - sus.
noth-ing but the blood of Je - sus.

*Refrain*

O pre cious is the flow that makes me white as snow;

no o - ther fount I know; noth-ing but the blood of Je - sus.

*Hymnary.org*

# December 11  Only His Righteousness

*...a righteous man...* James 5:16b

Yesterday, we looked at the meaning of fervent prayer. The next phrase in this verse says that it is the fervent prayer of a righteous man that avails much. So what is meant by a "righteous" man? (Let's clarify that the word "man" is generic, and includes both men and women, as in "mankind".)

We can be thankful James uses the word "righteous" and not *perfect*, since we could never qualify as *perfect*. It is impossible to be seen by God as righteous based on our own goodness. Isaiah reminds us that even what we see as our "righteousnesses" are filthy rags (Isaiah 64:6).

But since we have accepted the free gift of salvation that Jesus purchased for us, we can now be seen by God as righteous. When we approach God in prayer, He sees us covered, clothed with Jesus' white robe of righteousness. What a wonderfully reassuring image.

However, we still struggle with sin. I John 1:8-9 says "If we say that we have no sin, we deceive ourselves, and the truth is not in us." But "If we confess our sins, He is faithful and just to forgive us our sins, and to cleanse us from all unrighteousness." Acknowledging that we do have sin, confessing it and receiving forgiveness from Him are each necessary steps before we can move forward with a cleansed heart and renewed spirit. So, with David, let's ask God to "Create in me a clean heart, O God, and renew a steadfast spirit within me" (Psalm 51:10).

Let's come confidently before the Throne of Grace (Hebrews 4:16) with thanksgiving to Jesus for purchasing our perfect "robe of righteousness". Let's ask Him to show us how we may be soiling that white robe, and ask Him to enable us to walk blameless before Him.

**Today's Action:** Let's read Proverbs 11 together, letting His words of wisdom fall on good ground and bear much fruit for His kingdom.

*As righteousness leads to life, so he who pursues evil*
*pursues it to his own death. The fruit of the righteous*
*is a tree of life, and he who wins souls is wise.*
Proverbs 11:19, 30

# Sweet Hour Of Prayer

1. Sweet hour of prayer! sweet hour of prayer, That calls me from a world of care,
2. Sweet hour of prayer! sweet hour of prayer, Thy wings shall my pe - ti - tion bear
3. Sweet hour of prayer! sweet hour of prayer, May I thy con - so - la - tion share

And bids me at my Fa - ther's throne Make all my wants and wish - es known;
To Him whose truth and faith - ful - ness En - gage the wait - ing soul to bless;
Till, from Mount Pis - gah's loft - y height, I view my home, and take my flight;

In sea - sons of dis - tress and grief, My soul has oft - en found re - lief,
And since He bids me seek His face, Be - lieve His word, and trust His grace,
This robe of flesh I'll drop, and rise To seize the ev - er - last - ing prize;

And oft es - caped the tempt-er's snare, By thy re - turn, sweet hour of prayer.
I'll cast on Him my ev - 'ry care, And wait for Thee, sweet hour of prayer.
And shout, while pass - ing thru the air, Fare - well, fare - well sweet hour of prayer.

Words: W. W. Walford
Music: William B. Bradbury

# December 12                              Empowered

*...avails much.*   James 5:16b

After confessing our sins, receiving a cleansed heart and renewed spirit, and praying fervently, what results can we expect? What does it mean to *avail much?*

In II Corinthians 10:4-5, Paul declares "For the weapons of our warfare are not carnal, but mighty in God for pulling down strongholds; casting down arguments, and every high thing that exalts itself against the knowledge of God." What magnificent, powerful weaponry!

What are these weapons that are not carnal, but mighty through God? Prayer and the Word are the powerful weapons we have been given. Thankfully, their might is not dependent on the expert way in which we wield them. They are only mighty through God Almighty.

Our prayers can pull down strongholds in His people and our nation, as well as arguments that exalt themselves "against the knowledge of God." We may not know exactly what these strongholds and imaginations are, but God Almighty knows. And these are precisely what our mighty weapons were made to take on. Through God Almighty, we can expect them to accomplish much!

We have been called to this specific action at this specific time because our Good Shepherd is on the move, seeking out His sheep who have gone astray. How exciting it is that He has given us the privilege of partnering with Him through prayer to restore the hearts and lives of His people. If we, clothed in the righteousness of Jesus, pray fervently, we can enter this battle knowing that our prayers will *avail much*. Let us joyfully come before Him, rejoicing that He has invited us to partner with Him to revive His people and our nation.

**Today's Action:** Let's read Proverbs 12 together, asking Him to direct our hearts to receive His wisdom so our prayers will bring healing.

*The words of the reckless pierce like swords, but the tongue of the wise brings healing.* Proverbs 12:18 NIV

# Soldiers of Christ, Arise

1. Sol - diers of Christ, a - rise, And put your ar - mor on,
2. Stand, then, in His great might, With all His strength en - dued,
3. Leave no un - guard - ed place, No weak - ness of the soul,

Strong in the strength which God sup - plies Thru His e - ter - nal Son.
And take, to arm you for the fight, The *pan - o - ply of God!
Take eve - ry vir - tue, eve - ry grace, And for - ti - fy the whole.

Strong in the Lord of Hosts, And in His might - y pow'r,
That, hav - ing all things done, And all your con - flicts past,
From strength to strength go on; Wres - tle, and fight, and pray;

Who in the strength of Je - sus trusts Is more than con - quer - or.
Ye may o'er - come thru Christ a - lone, And stand en - tire at last.
Tread all the pow'rs of dark - ness down, And win the well-fought day! A - men.

*(vs. 2) panoply: a full suit of armor

Words: Charles Wesley (1749)
Music: Sir George Job Elvey (1868)

# December 13                                    Battle Ready

*Put on the whole armor of God, that you may be able to stand*
*against the schemes of the devil.*                     Ephesians 6:11 ESV

Let's be careful not to take this battle on too lightly. This is war! Our enemy is deadly serious about this battle for the hearts and souls of God's people and our nation. Therefore, so should we.

We are joining together all across this nation in spiritual battle. We have declared war, so we should expect opposition. It is beyond foolish to think the enemy of our souls is just going to walk away without a fight.

We have been given a full suit of armor so we can stand firm in this fight. Ephesians 6:12-13 reminds us that we are not fighting "against flesh and blood, but against principalities, against powers, against the rulers of the darkness of this age, against spiritual hosts of wickedness in the heavenly places. Therefore take up the whole armor of God, that you may be able to withstand in the evil day, and having done all, to stand."

We are instructed to put on the full armor of God so we can stand against the deceptions, the tricks, and the schemes of the devil. Therefore, we would be wise to heed and follow that instruction.

Over the next few days, we will examine each piece of our armor so we can stand firm in our fight against the enemy and his forces of evil who have been unleashed on and in our nation. Sound scary? Only if we were going it alone and in our own strength. But we are fighting in the power of His might, with the victory already assured because of Jesus!

Let's come before His throne together today, thankful for all the many truths He has given us in His Word that allow us to take a victorious stand against the enemy and his evil forces.

**Today's Action:** Let's read Proverbs 13 together, with a heart full of faith and commitment to follow our Commander's instructions as we gear up for battle.

*He who despises the word will be destroyed,*
*but he who fears the commandment will be rewarded.*
Proverbs 13:13

# Standing On The Promises

1. Stand-ing on the prom-is-es of Christ my King, Thru e-ter-nal ag-es
2. Stand-ing on the prom-is-es that can-not fail, When the howl-ing storms of
3. Stand-ing on the prom-is-es I now can see; Per-fect, pre-sent cleans-ing
4. Stand-ing on the prom-is-es of Christ the Lord, Bound to Him e-ter-nal-
5. Stand-ing on the prom-is-es I can-not fall, List'n-ing ev-'ry mo-ment

let His prais-es ring; Glo-ry in the high-est, I will shout and sing,
doubt and fear as-sail, By the liv-ing word of God I shall pre-vail,
in the blood for me; Stand-ing in the lib-er-ty where Christ makes free,
ly by love's strong cord, O-ver-com-ing dai-ly with the Spir-it's sword,
to the Spir-it's call, Rest-ing in my Sav-ior, as my all in all,

**Chorus**

Stand-ing on the prom-is-es of God. Stand - ing, stand - ing,
Stand-ing on the prom-is-es, stand-ing on the prom-is-es,

Stand-ing on the prom-is-es of God my Sav-ior; Stand - ing,
Stand-ing on the prom-is-es,

stand - ing, I'm stand-ing on the prom-is-es of God.
stand-ing on the prom-is-es,

Words and Music: R. Kelso Carter

# December 14                                    Belt of Truth

*Stand firm then, with the belt of truth buckled around your waist...*
                                                    Ephesians 6:14 NIV

The purpose of putting God's armor on is so we can stand against the schemes and deceptions of the enemy. Therefore, it's most important to start by arming ourselves with God's truth. Only *His* truth can expose and destroy the enemy's deceptions.

In the Roman soldiers' suit of armor, the first thing they put on was their belt. Then they would tuck the end of their tunic up under their belt. This immediately increased their mobility by freeing their legs from being tripped up by their clothing.[8] If attacked by the enemy before they could get their hands on any other gear, the belt would at least allow them to run to safety if necessary. That's why our belt is listed first in our armor.

Why a belt of truth? Have you heard the phrase "gird your loins"? It means to prepare for action. If we gird our loins with His truth, it is easier to identify the opposite - the lies with which Satan tries to trip us up.

To be girded with truth, we first need to know *The Truth*, our Lord and Savior, Jesus Christ (John 14:6). Then, because God's Word is truth (John 17:17), we need to be firmly grounded in His Word, totally committed to who He is, to what He has said, and to what He can do.

Let's ask our God to help us securely buckle our belt of truth today. Let's remind Him and ourselves of some of that truth: that He alone is God Almighty; He alone hears and answers prayer; He alone knows the beginning from the end; He alone works all things together for the good of those who love Him. These truths can firmly set our minds to battle.

**Today's Action:** Let's read Proverbs 14 together, and ask Him to show us any ways that may seem right to us, but actually are the devil's deadly lies and deceptions poisoning our hearts and minds. Then let's commit to stand firmly in the truth.

*There is a way that seems right to a man,*
*but its end is the way of death.*
                    Proverbs 14:12

# My Jesus, I Love Thee

1. My Je - sus I love Thee, I know Thou art mine;
2. I love Thee be - cause Thou hast first lov - ed me,
3. I'll love Thee in life, I will love Thee in death,
4. In man - sions of glo - ry and end - less de - light,

For Thee, all the fol - lies of sin I re - sign;
And pur - chased my par - don on Cal - va - ry's tree;
And praise Thee as long as Thou lend - est me breath;
I'll e - ver a - dore Thee in hea - ven so bright.

My gra - cious Re - dee - mer, my Sa - vior art Thou;
I love Thee for wear - ing the thorns on Thy brow;
And say, when the death dew lies cold on my brow;
And sing - ing Thy prai - ses, be - fore Thee I'll bow;

If e - ver I loved Thee, my Je - sus, 'tis now.
If e - ver I loved Thee, my Je - sus, 'tis now.
If e - ver I loved Thee, my Je - sus, 'tis now.
If e - ver I loved Thee, my Je - sus, 'tis now.

Text: William R. Featherston, 1846-1873
Tune: Adoniram J. Gordon, 1836-1895

11 11 11 11
GORDON
www.hymnary.org/text/my_jesus_i_love_thee_i_know_thou_art_mi

# December 15    Breastplate of Rightcousness

*...having put on the breastplate of righteousness...*Ephesians 6:14

After our belt of truth is secure, we can ask ourselves "Now, what's our most vulnerable place?" It's our heart. That's why the breastplate is our second piece of armor we put on.

What is our "breastplate of righteousness"? Thankfully, it is not a breastplate of our own righteousness, which Isaiah describes as filthy rags (Isaiah 64:6). Through faith, our breastplate is made of the righteousness of God through Jesus (II Corinthians 5:21).

The Roman soldier's breastplate was made of bronze or chain mail and had loops or buckles that attached it to the belt, both front and back. The weight was then carried by the belt and not the soldier's shoulders.[9] Our shoulders don't have to carry the weight of providing our righteousness. We can rest in the perfect provision of His.

In Philippians 3:9, Paul said he wanted to "be found in Him, not having my own righteousness, which is from the law, but that which is through faith in Christ, the righteousness which is from God by faith." An online writer for gotquestions.org put it this way: "The breastplate of righteousness has Christ's name stamped on it, as though He said, 'Your righteousness isn't sufficient to protect you. Wear mine.' " [10]

Let's thank Jesus for providing us His breastplate of righteousness to protect our hearts, and ask Him to expose anything in our lives that might mar His perfect breastplate. Then let's confess, repent and be cleansed so that no sin tarnishes this costly, perfect breastplate He has given us.

**Today's action:** Let's read Proverbs 15 together, letting this chapter's words shine a light into our open, redeemed hearts so our prayers will be a delight to Him.

*The sacrifice of the wicked is an abomination to the LORD,*
*but the prayer of the upright is His delight. The LORD is far*
*from the wicked, but He hears the prayer of the righteous.*
Proverbs 15:8, 29

# I Love To Tell The Story

1. I love to tell the sto - ry Of un - seen things a - bove, Of
2. I love to tell the sto - ry; More won - der - ful it seems Than
3. I love to tell the sto - ry; 'Tis pleas - ant to re - peat What
4. I love to tell the sto - ry, For those who know it best Seem

Je - sus and His glo - ry, Of Je - sus and His love; I love to
all the gold - en fan - cies Of all my gold - en dreams; I love to
seems, each time I tell it, More won - der - ful - ly sweet; I love to
hun - ger - ing and thirst - ing To hear it like the rest; And when, in

tell the sto - ry Be - cause I know 'tis true; It sat - is - fies my
tell the sto - ry; It did so much for me; And that is just the
tell the sto - ry, For some have nev - er heard The mes - sage of sal -
scenes of glo - ry, I sing the new, new song, 'Twill be the old, old

*Chorus*

long - ings As noth - ing else can do.
rea - son I tell it now to thee. I love to tell the sto - ry! 'Twill
va - tion From God's own ho - ly word.
sto - ry That I have loved so long.

be my theme in glo - ry To tell the old, old sto - ry Of Je - sus and His love.

Words by Catherine Hankey
Music by William G. Fischer

PDHymns.com

# December 16                    "Good News Shoes"

*...and having shod your feet with the preparation of the gospel of peace.*                                      Ephesians 6:15

"Having shod your feet with the preparation of the gospel of peace" is a phrase that doesn't create a very clear image, so let's break it down a bit.

The Roman soldiers' feet were fitted or "shod" with military-grade sandals. Straps were attached to the sole which crisscrossed the foot and then tied up around the ankle. This created a secure sole, which was spiked to give a firm grip on slippery terrain. This footwear helped them not only hold their ground, but more easily gain ground when called to advance in battle. In the same way, our "good news shoes" can help us stand firm, as well as advance, against our enemy.

The phrase "with the preparation" is similar to the instruction in II Timothy 4:2 and I Peter 3:15 to be prepared at all times, both in and out of season, to share the *good news* of the hope that is in us. We should have the *good news* of peace with God always front and center. This focus will also strengthen us with firm conviction as we do battle.

The "gospel of peace" is the *good news* that we can have reconciliation and peace with God through Jesus' death and resurrection. This peace with God is secure through all eternity, and through all of life's *unpeaceful* circumstances. Now that's good news!

Let's thank the Lord that no matter how much of our world gives way, He has everything under control. His plan cannot be thwarted by the enemy. Let's lace up our "good news shoes" so we will always be prepared to share His *good news*. But let's also stop to seek His wisdom and His direction about how, when and what to speak into another person's life. He promises to give us the right words at the right time.

**Today's Action:** Let's read Proverbs 16 together, with a heart thirsty for His words of wisdom to speak into the lives of others.

*To humans belong the plans of the heart, but from the LORD comes the proper answer of the tongue.*
Proverbs 16:1 NIV

# Faith Is the Victory

John Henry Yates, 1891

Ira David Sankey

1. En - camped a - long the hills of light, Ye Christ - ian sol - diers, rise. And press the bat - tle
2. His ban - ner o - ver us is love, Our sword the Word of God. We tread the road the
3. On ev - ery hand the foe we find Drawn up in dread ar - ray. Let tents of ease be
4. To him that o - ver - comes the foe, White rai - ment shall be giv'n. Be - fore the an - gels

ere the night Shall veil the glow - ing skies. A - gainst the foe in vales be - low Let
saints a - bove With shouts of tri - umph trod. By faith, they like a whirl - wind's breath, Swept
left be - hind. And on - ward to the fray. Sal - va - tion's hel - met on each head, With
he shall know His name con - fessed in heav'n. Then on - ward from the hill of light, Our

all our strength be hurled. Faith is the vic - to - ry, we know, That o - ver - comes the world.
on o'er ev - ery field. The faith by which they con - quered death Is still our shin - ing shield.
truth all girt a - bout, The earth shall trem - ble 'neath our tread, And e - cho with our shout.
hearts with love a - flame, We'll van - quish all the hosts of night, In Je - sus con - qu'ring name.

**Refrain**

Faith is the vic - to - ry! Faith is the vic - to - ry! O glor - i - ous vic - to - ry, that o - ver - comes the world.

# December 17        Shield of Faith

*...above all, taking the shield of faith with which you will be able to quench all the fiery darts of the wicked one.*    Ephesians 6:16

The Roman soldier's shield was intentionally large. It was designed so the soldier could crouch down and hide behind it, if necessary. Groups of soldiers could also gather together and put their shields above and around themselves, forming a "tortoise shell" of protection.

Our shield of faith can also give us a place of refuge, a place of protection, a place of rest. When things are looking out of control, our faith confirms that *none* of this is a surprise to our God. He is still on His throne, and He *will* accomplish His will, for our good and for the furthering of His purposes.

Paul also describes our shield of faith as an effective fire extinguisher, quenching "all the fiery darts of the wicked one." Flaming arrows were the most powerful weapons of Roman warfare. So a wise soldier would soak his shield in water before battle to keep fiery darts from setting it on fire.

In the same way, we are wise to keep our hearts and minds soaked in the living water of the Word. Then our shield of faith can extinguish *all* of our enemy's flaming arrows. Our enemy may think his fiery darts of doubt, fear or temptation are powerful. But our Word-soaked shield of faith is greater still.

Our weapons of warfare are too powerful for our enemy and he knows it. If only we knew it. He only wins if we get distracted, lay down our weapons, or if we never even enter the fight. So let's fight! Victory is ours! After all, faith is the victory that overcomes the world! (I John 5:4)

**Today's Action:** Let's read Proverbs 17 together, asking Him to help us see life's circumstances through our eyes of faith, which can give us a cheerful heart and protect us from a broken spirit.

> *A merry heart does good, like medicine,*
> *but a broken spirit dries the bones.*
> Proverbs 17:22

# I Stand Amazed in the Presence

1. I stand a-mazed in the pre – sence Of Je – sus the Na – za – rene,
2. For me it was in the gar – den He prayed,"Not my will, but Thine,"
3. He took my sins and my sor – rows, He made them His ve – ry own;
4. When with the ran-somed in glo – ry His face I at last shall see,

And won – der how He could love me, A sin – ner, con-demned, un – clean.
He had no tears for His own griefs, But sweat drops of blood for mine.
He bore the bur – den to Cal – v'ry, And suf – fered and died a – lone.
"Twill be my joy thro' the a – ges To sing of His love for me.

How mar – ve-lous! how won-der-ful! And my song shall e – ver be;
Oh, how mar-vel-ous! oh, how won-der-ful!

How mar – ve-lous! how won-der-ful! Is my__ Sa – vior's love for me!
Oh, how mar-vel-ous! oh, how won-der-ful!

Text: Charles H. Gabriel, 1856-1932
Tune: Charles H. Gabriel, 1856-1932

87 87 Refrain
MY SAVIOR'S LOVE
www.hymnary.org/text/i_stand_amazed_in_the_presence

# December 18                    Helmet of Salvation

*And take the helmet of salvation...* Ephesians 6:17

The purpose of a helmet is to protect a soldier's head. But in this metaphor, our helmet of salvation is issued to protect our minds. While our breastplate of righteousness specifically protects our hearts, our helmet of salvation specifically protects our minds.

How does salvation protect our minds? Our salvation gives us reconciliation, peace with God. Philippians 4:7 says "And the peace of God, which surpasses all understanding, will guard your hearts and your minds through Christ Jesus." The peace of God protects our minds. Our minds can be at rest in the midst of any circumstance because our salvation is an accomplished fact; it is secure for all eternity.

Referring to His sheep, Jesus said "I give them eternal life, and they shall never perish; neither shall anyone snatch them out of My hand" (John 10:28). As His sheep who hear and follow His voice, our redemption, our salvation, is secure forever. May we stand amazed that He has chosen us; that He has redeemed us; that no man can pluck us out of His hand. May this assurance protect our minds as we prepare to engage in battle with the great deceiver. Because of the substitutionary death and resurrection of Jesus Christ, our ultimate victory is assured.

Let's come into His presence today, thankful that we have been given a helmet of salvation to guard our minds. Let's ask Him to help us keep our minds sharp, being sober and watchful, because our enemy is always on the prowl looking for moments of weakness (1 Peter 5:8). Let's ask God to confirm to us the security and surety of our salvation, and then use that as a truth point to expose our enemy's deceptions and schemes.

**Today's Action:** Let's read Proverbs 18 together, committed to challenging the great deceiver's deceptions, exposing his lies in our lives so we can walk in integrity and truth.

*The first one to plead his case seems right, until*
*another comes and cross-examines him.*
Proverbs 18:17 AMP

# Holy Bible, Book Divine

1. Ho - ly Bi - ble, Book di - vine, Pre - cious trea - sure,
2. Mine_ to chide me when I rove, Mine to show a
3. Mine_ to com - fort in_ dis - tress, Suff' - ring in this
4. Mine_ to tell of joys_ to come, And_ the re - bel

thou_ art mine: Mine to tell me whence I
Sa - vior's love; Mine thou art to guide and
wil - der - ness; Mine to show, by li - ving
sin - ner's doom: O thou ho - ly Book di -

came; Mine_ to teach me what_ I am.
guard; Mine_ to pu - nish or_ re - ward.
faith, We_ can tri - umph o - ver death.
vine, Pre - cious trea - sure, thou_ art mine.

*Hymnary.org*

# December 19                                    The Sword

*...and the sword of the Spirit, which is the word of God.* Eph. 6:17

T oday, let's look at our last physical piece of armor, our sword, which is clearly defined as the word of God. This image is repeated again in Hebrews 4:12: "For the word of God is living and powerful, and sharper than any two-edged sword, piercing even to the division of soul and spirit, and of joints and marrow; and is a discerner of the thoughts and intents of the heart." Sharper than a two-edged sword. That's powerful!

Out of our six physical pieces of armor – our belt, breastplate, shoes, shield, helmet, and sword - the sword is the only piece that can be used for offense. The rest is for defense. This tells us God takes our protection seriously, so *we* should take our protection seriously. It has been provided to us, so we are foolish not to use it. Why? Because the devil "prowls around like a roaring lion seeking someone to devour" (I Peter 5:8 AMP).

We would also be well-advised to follow Jesus' example when He effectively fought Satan's temptations in the wilderness. As described in Matthew 4 and Luke 4, Jesus responded to each of Satan's temptations with "It is written...", quoting the Word. God Himself quoted the Word, who could have destroyed Satan with just one breath! How much more should we value His Word, our powerful weapon of the sword of truth.

Interestingly, the ever-clever Satan took note and quoted Scripture in the last of his temptations, so he is also aware of the Word. We shouldn't be surprised then when the Word gets misquoted and misapplied. It is all part of our adversary's clever schemes. All the more reason to keep our swords sharpened by diligent, deep study of God's Holy Word. Let's thank the Lord for giving us the powerful weapon of His Word, and ask Him to create an insatiable hunger and thirst for more of it in our daily lives. May we see it as our only source of truth to counter the devil's lies.

**Today's Action:** Let's read Proverbs 19 together with a teachable spirit, willing to receive and apply the instruction and correction it offers.

*Cease listening to instruction, my son, and you will stray from the words of knowledge.* Proverbs 19:27

# What a Friend We Have in Jesus

1. What a friend we have in Je - sus, All our sins and griefs to bear!
2. Have we tri - als and temp - ta - tions? Is there trou - ble a - ny - where?
3. Are we weak and hea - vy la - den, Cum - bered with a load of care?

What a pri - vi - lege to car - ry Ev' - ry - thing to God in prayer!
We should ne - ver be dis - cour - aged, Take it to the Lord in prayer:
Pre - cious Sa - vior, still our re - fuge; Take it to the Lord in prayer:

Oh, what peace we of - ten for - feit, Oh, what need - less pain we bear,
Can we find a friend so faith - ful Who will all our sor - rows share?
Do thy friends des - pise, for - sake thee? Take it to the Lord in prayer;

All be - cause we do not car - ry Ev' - ry - thing to God in prayer!
Je - sus knows our ev' - ry weak - ness, Take it to the Lord in prayer!
In His arms He'll take and shield thee; Thou wilt find a so - lace there.

Text: Joseph Scriven, 1819-1886
Tune: Charles C. Converse, 1832-1918

87 87D
CONVERSE
www.hymnary.org/text/what_a_friend_we_have_in_jesus_all_our_s

*And pray in the Spirit on all occasions with all kinds of prayers and requests...be alert and always keep on praying...*    Ephesians 6:18 NIV

Paul ends his discourse on the armor of God with the words "and pray...on all occasions...with all kinds of prayers and requests...and always keep on praying...". It is reasonable to suggest then that prayer and our sword (the Word) are our two offensive pieces of weaponry.

Paul describes our weapons as "not carnal, but mighty in God for pulling down strongholds" (II Corinthians 10:4). Pulling down strongholds! Sounds like mighty powerful weaponry we have been given.

What makes our prayers powerful? The length of time or the words we say? No. Our prayers are only mighty "through God" (KJV). He takes our prayers and petitions and empowers them with His power, His authority, His might. Our prayers are powerful not because of *how*, but *to whom*, we pray. That lifts a lot of the performance pressure, doesn't it? We simply need to be faithful to pray as He directs. And we know He will be faithful to answer – in His time, in His way, and in His plan.

Let's also keep in mind that the purpose of prayer is not to *change* the will of God; it is to *accomplish* the will of God. Therefore, we need to be frequently checking in with headquarters to make sure we are on the same page as our Commander. We need to seek His face, listen for His direction and follow His advice and guidance as we wage this war.

Let's approach the Throne of Grace today, thankful for the mind-blowing fact that we can talk one-on-one with the God of the Universe. We have the privilege of seeking His face, receiving His advice and guidance for effective warfare in order to advance.

**Today's Action:** Let's intently read every word of Proverbs 20, with a focus to search out and apply those corrections and instructions that are most needed in our own lives.

*Plans are established by seeking advice;*
*so if you wage war, obtain guidance.*
Proverbs 20:18 NIV

# Lead On, O King Eternal

1. Lead on, O King E - ter - nal, The day of march has come;
2. Lead on, O King E - ter - nal, Till sin's fierce war shall cease,
3. Lead on, O King E - ter - nal, We fol - low not with fears;

Hence - forth in fields of con - quest Thy tents shall be our home:
And ho - li - ness shall whis - per The sweet a - men of peace;
For glad - ness breaks like mor - ning Wher - e'er Thy face ap - pears;

Thro' days of pre - pa - ra - tion Thy grace has made us strong,___
For not with swords' loud clash - ing, Or roll of stir - ring drums;___
Thy cross is lif - ted o'er___ us; We jour - ney in its light:___

And now, O King E - ter - nal, We lift our bat - tle song.
With deeds of love and mer - cy The heav'n - ly king - dom comes.
The crown a - waits the con - quest; Lead on, O God of might.

Text: Ernest W. Shurtleff, 1862-1917
Tune: Henry T. Smart, 1813-1879

76 76D
LANCASHIRE
www.hymnary.org/text/lead_on_o_king_eternal_the_day_of_march

# December 21                    Wielding our Weapons

*For the weapons of our warfare are not of the flesh but have divine power to destroy strongholds.*                    II Corinthians 10:4 ESV

W e have been given two weapons that not only protect us defensively from our enemy's attacks, but they can also be used offensively, having "divine power to destroy strongholds." These two weapons are prayer and our sword - God's Word.

Why is prayer considered one of our weapons? It's not in the armor list, is it? Well, it actually is, but not as a physical piece of armor we put on. It is a weapon that we use along with our sword. After instructing us to put on all the physical pieces of our armor, including "the sword of the Spirit, which is the word of God", Paul continues with this instruction: "...and pray...on all occasions...with all kinds of prayers and requests" (Ephesians 6:18 NIV). Clearly, prayer is an essential part of our arsenal.

How do we wield our weapons of prayer and our sword, the Word? They actually work very well together. Our prayers can include praying His Word to Him, recounting His promises, reaffirming His truth. This not only reminds us to pray according to His will, but it also strengthens our faith because we are reminding ourselves of His truth in the process.

What can that look like? We can, for example, declare His promise that His Word will not return void (Isaiah 55:11); we can ask Him to give His people a pure heart and renew a right spirit in us (Psalm 51:10); we can pray that, as Lord of the harvest, He would send reapers (Matt 9:38).

He has promised to lead, if we will ask and then heed. Let's ask the Lord today to help us learn to effectively wield our weapons of prayer and His Word, listening to His leading and direction in this battle. He knows what strongholds we should ask His forces to demolish.

**Today's Action:** With a humble and teachable heart, let's together read Proverbs 21, asking Him to reveal strongholds He wants to destroy.

*One who is wise can go up against the city of the mighty and pull down the stronghold in which they trust.*
Proverbs 21:22 NIV

# Onward Christian Soldiers

1. On - ward, Chris - tian sol - diers! March - ing as to war, With the cross of
2. At the sign of tri - umph, Sa - tan's host doth flee; On, then Chris - tian
3. Like a might - y ar - my Moves the Church of God: Broth-ers, we are
4. Crowns and thrones may per - ish, King - doms rise and wane, But the church of
5. On - ward, then, ye peo - ple, Join our hap - py throng; Blend with ours your

Je - sus Go - ing on be - fore; Christ, the roy - al Mas - ter. Leads a -
sol - diers, On to vic - to - ry; Hell's foun - da - tions quiv - er At the
tread - ing Where the saints have trod, We are not di - vid - ed, All one
Je - sus Con - stant will re - main; Gates of hell can nev - er 'Gainst that
voic - es In the tri - umph song; Glo - ry, laud and hon - or Un - to

*Chorus*

gainst the foe; For - ward in - to bat - tle, See His ban - ners go!
shout of praise; Bro-thers, lift your voic - es, Loud your an - themsraise!
bod - y we: One in hope and doc - trine, One in char - i - ty. On-ward,Chris-tian
church pre - vail; This thru count-less a - ges Men and an - gels sing.
Christ the King, This thru count-less ag - es Men and an - gels sing.

sol - diers! March - ing as to war, With the cross of Je - sus Go-ing on be - fore.

Words by Sabine Baring-Gould
Music by Arthur Sullivan

# December 22                                          Suit Up!

How foolish we would be to learn all about our armor and then just admire it. We are instructed to put it on. We are in a battle, so we need to suit up. But how do we do that?

Paul doesn't say precisely how we put it on, so it's probably not important *how* we put it on; it's important *that* we put it on. We can thank the Lord every morning for each piece as we visualize them, for example, asking His help to use them as He leads. Or we can say "I put on my belt of truth", and then thank Him for each piece. We can remind ourselves at any time of day or night about each amazing piece of our armor, asking Him to make sure that our "belt of truth" is securely buckled, that He will show us things that we may be thinking or doing that might tarnish His "breastplate of righteousness", etc.

Hand motions can help to remember what the pieces of our armor are. The first three – our belt, breastplate and shoes – require two hands to put on, so those go on first – hands on hips for belt, on chest for breastplate, then point to our feet to "put on" our shoes. Then "pick up" our shield with our left hand, "put on" our helmet with our right hand, then use our now-free right hand to "pick up" our sword. Now, with prayer, we are fully armed and battle-ready!

A prudent person recognizes danger and prepares for it. So let's make sure we are fully protected in our amazing suit of God's armor at all times. The most important thing to remember about each piece of armor is that each one is grounded in His Word. Let's make sure our ideas about truth, righteousness, the gospel, faith, and salvation continue to line up with His Word. And when we feel particularly under attack, let's immerse ourselves all that much more in His Word. Then let's thank Him for His provision and the privilege of joining in His battle to accomplish His will.

**Today's Action:** Let's read Proverbs 22 together, with hearts that seek His correction and direction, so we can be more effective warriors.

*A prudent and far-sighted person sees the evil of sin and hides himself from it, but the naïve continue on and are punished by suffering the consequences of sin.*          Proverbs 22:3 AMP

# My Faith Looks Up to Thee

1. My faith looks up to Thee, Thou Lamb of Cal - va - ry,
2. May Thy rich grace im - part Strength to my faint - ing heart,
3. While life's dark maze I tread, And griefs a - round me spread,
4. When ends life's tran - sient dream, When death's cold, sul - len stream

Sa - vior di - vine! Now hear me while I pray, Take all my
My zeal in - spire; As Thou hast died for me, O may my
Be Thou my guide; Bid dark - ness turn to day, Wipe sor - row's
Shall o'er me roll, Blest Sa - vior, then, in love, Fear and dis -

guilt a - way, O let me from this day Be whol - ly Thine!
love to Thee Pure, warm, and change - less be A li - ving fire.
tears a - way, Nor let me e - ver stray From Thee a - side.
trust re - move; O bear me safe a - bove, A ran - somed soul!

Text: Ray Palmer, 1808-1887
Tune: Lowell Mason, 1792-1872

Irregular
OLIVET
www.hymnary.org/text/my_faith_looks_up_to_thee

# December 23                    The Dart of Doubt

Paul says our shield of faith effectively extinguishes Satan's fiery darts, so let's talk about one of his most effective darts – doubt. It worked when he asked Eve, "Did God really say...?" (Genesis 3:1 NIV). If only she had responded with truth, we wouldn't be in such trouble.

When Satan tries to distract us with doubt, one of the best extinguishing truths is "In the beginning God..." (Genesis 1:1). When doubt tries to creep in, counter with the creation. Go outside and look at the stars. There are so many stars, we don't even know how many there are. Yet, the Word says He calls them all by name. It takes our breath away. The universe could not have just happened! There has to be a God!

If it's daytime, examine the unbelievable intricacies of nature. Watch the tiny ants as they scurry about, touching their antennae as they communicate some kind of message and hurry on their way. Or watch a spider become aware of your presence and race off to find the nearest hiding place. How can there be "thinking" skills in such tiny little creatures? There has to be a Creator!

Or re-read the account of how God rescued the Israelites out of Egypt (Exodus 7-14). This account was written by Moses who actually witnessed those amazing signs and wonders! They really happened! There has to be a God who created, and is actively involved with His creation. That same God is the same yesterday, today, and forever (Hebrews 13:8).

Let's remind ourselves of His truths that are especially meaningful to each of us. Grounded in the truth of His Word, let's gird our loins, prepared to stand firm in this, His battle. Let's ask Him to help us detect and douse those fiery darts of doubt. Then let's pray confidently in renewed faith, knowing our prayers have been answered even if we don't ever get to see it, because we walk by faith and not by sight (II Cor. 5:7).

**Today's Action:** Let's read Proverbs 23 together, turning our back on doubt, and choosing to apply His instruction to our hearts and minds today.

*Apply your heart to instruction and your ears*
*to words of knowledge.*     Proverbs 23:12

# Bring Them In

1. Hark! 'tis the Shep-herd's voice I hear, Out in the de - sert dark and drear,
2. Who'll go and help this Shep-herd kind, Help Him the wan - d'ring ones to find?
3. Out in the de - sert hear their cry Out on the moun - tains wild and high;

Call - ing the sheep who've gone a - stray Far from the Shep-herd's fold a - way.
Who'll bring the lost ones to the fold, Where they'll be shel - tered from the cold?
Hark! 'tis the Mas - ter speaks to thee, "Go find My sheep wher - e'er they be."

*Chorus*

Bring them in, bring them in, Bring them in from the fields of sin;

Bring them in, bring them in, Bring the wan - d'ring ones to Je - sus.

Words by Alexcenah Thomas
Music by William A. Ogden

# December 24                                    The Triangle

Communication. It can be one of the greatest challenges of life. Often communication can turn into a verbal competition instead. We end up talking *at* each other instead of *with* each other.

Visualize a triangle. When two people are across from each other on the bottom line of that triangle trying to communicate, it can become a "boxing match". While a gentle answer can turn away wrath (Proverbs 15:1), conflict can remain because it becomes less about the topic and more a matter of the heart. And only God can change hearts.

Visualize God at the top of a triangle. We can send our concerns up the triangle to God in prayer, and ask Him to work down the sides of the triangle to work change in our hearts. Once we ask God to handle it, we can let it go. We then can be less stressed, as we choose to trust Him.

The visual of a triangle can also help demonstrate the power of prayer. The power of prayer is not found in the prayers we send up to God; it is only found in His powerful answers coming back down. That's why Paul can say that our weapons are "mighty *through God* to the pulling down of strongholds" (II Cor. 10:4 KJV – emphasis added).

This triangle concept is also consistent with Jesus' teaching in Matthew 9:37-38: "The harvest is plentiful but the laborers are few. Therefore, pray the Lord of the harvest, to send out laborers into His harvest." He didn't tell us to go make others work the harvest. That could end up in fisticuffs, or we could end up trying to do it in our own power.

Instead, Jesus says to pray that the *Lord* would send workers. Our role is to pray; His role is to call, equip and send. We may be the reapers that He sends, but the sending is up to Him. So let's come before Him, asking Him to bring the hearts of His people and our nation back to Him, and then follow His guidance as He leads us into battle for His purposes.

**Today's Action:** Let's read Proverbs 24 together, seeking guidance so that we can help bring about the victorious harvest He has planned.

*Surely you need guidance to wage war,*
*and victory is won through many advisers.*
Proverbs 24:6 NIV

# O Come, All Ye Faithful

Text: Latin hymn;
    ascribed to John Francis Wade, c.1710-1786;
    tr. Frederick Oakeley, 1802-1880 and others
Tune: John Frances Wade, c. 1710-1786

Irregular
ADESTE FIELES

# December 25                                    Yielding

*The LORD is my strength and my shield; my heart trusted in*
*Him, and I am helped; therefore, my heart greatly rejoices, and with*
*my song I will praise Him.*                         Psalm 28:7

This verse makes an excellent framework for prayer. If we start by recognizing that He alone is our strength and shield, we can more willingly yield our spirit to His control to be used for His purposes. We can more readily accept that His ways are higher than our ways. We can more easily focus our hearts on having Him alone be our heart's desire.

It's so natural for us to have the focus on ourselves, isn't it? After all, our individual minds are being carried around inside our individual bodies 24-7. We are inclined to think about ourselves all the time, constantly checking in on ourselves. "How do I feel? Am I hungry or thirsty? Am I too hot or too cold? Do I feel loved, appreciated, valued?" We sometimes think that only after we check the boxes that all is fine in *our* world, then we might have some time leftover to give to God or to others.

In contrast, this Psalm directs us to speak truth to our *self*, who naturally is *self*-ish and *self*-focused. The truth reminds our *self* that we are not our own strength; we are not our own shield. We are wise to yield our spirits to Him alone, to trust in Him alone. We can turn our focus from ourselves and make Him and His kingdom the focus of our hearts. Then, and only then, can our hearts be emptied of *self* and be filled with His joy and love. And then we will long to praise and worship Him alone.

This is Christmas Day. Let's bow in humble worship to the King of kings. May we rededicate our lives for His use, asking Him to remove the dross from the silver so we can be useful vessels for Him in His kingdom plans and purposes.

**Today's Action:** Let's read Proverbs 25 together, submitting to His refining fire, so we can be used to bring more honor and glory to Him.

*Remove the dross from the silver,*
*and a silversmith can produce a vessel.*
Proverbs 25:4 NIV

# Take Time to Be Holy

1. Take time to be ho-ly, Speak oft with thy Lord; A-bide in Him al-ways, And feed on his Word; Make friends of God's chil-dren, Help those who are weak; For-get-ting in noth-ing His bles-sing to seek.

2. Take time to be ho-ly, The world rush-es on; Spend much time in se-cret With Je-sus a-lone; By look-ing to Je-sus Like Him thou shalt be; Thy friends in thy con-duct His like-ness shall see.

3. Take time to be ho-ly, Let Him be thy guide, And run not be-fore Him What-ev-er be-tide; In joy or in sor-row Still fol-low thy Lord, And look-ing to Je-sus, Still trust in His Word.

4. Take time to be ho-ly, Be calm in thy soul; Each tho't and each mo-tive Be-neath His con-trol; Thus led by His Spi-rit To foun-tains of love, Thou soon shalt be fit-ted For ser-vice a-bove.

Text: William D. Longstaff, 1822-1894
Tune: George C. Stebbins, 1846-1945

65 65D
HOLINESS
www.hymnary.org/text/take_time_to_be_holy

# December 26                           Blind Spot

*Search me, O God, and know my heart;...see if there is any wicked way in me, and lead me in the way everlasting.*      Psalm 139:23-24

If we have spent any time behind the wheel of a car, we all have experienced the shock of the "Blind Spot". How is it possible that an entire vehicle can be hidden from our view? And what devastating consequences for us and others if we ignore its reality.

The same can be true in our own lives. Jesus asks us in Matthew 7:3 - "Why do you look at the speck of sawdust in your brother's eye and pay no attention to the plank in your own eye?" Talk about a blind spot!

No one wants to be called a hypocrite. But that is precisely the word that Jesus uses to describe us when we criticize others, but refuse to acknowledge and deal with our own obvious "plank".

The first important factor regarding blind spots is to acknowledge that they exist. Without exceptional effort, we are truly blind to what is there. We need to ask the Lord to reveal to us our blind spots, those areas in our hearts and minds that we simply cannot see on our own. We need Him to give us the miracle of His clear sight.

Let's humbly come before His Throne of Grace and ask Him to reveal the blind spots in our hearts and minds, where we may be seeing ourselves as *wise in our own eyes*. Then let's ask Him to lead us in repentance and put us back on track, for profitable use in His kingdom and for His glory.

**Today's Action:** Let's read Proverbs 26 together, with a thirst for His truth and a willingness to yield our spirit to His control, His correction and His direction.

*Do you see a man wise in his own eyes?*
*There is more hope for a fool than for him.*
Proverbs 26:12

# I Need Thee Every Hour

1. I need Thee ev'ry hour, Most gra - cious Lord;
2. I need Thee ev'ry hour, Stay Thou near - by;
3. I need Thee ev'ry hour, In joy or pain;
4. I need Thee ev'ry hour, Teach me Thy will;
5. I need Thee ev'ry hour, Most Ho - ly One;

No ten - der voice like Thine Can peace af - ford.
Temp - ta - tions lose their pow'r When Thou art nigh.
Come quick - ly and a - bide, Or life is vain.
Thy pro - mi - ses so rich In me ful - fill.
O make me Thine in - deed, Thou bles - sed Son

I need Thee, O I need Thee; Ev' - ry hour I need Thee!

O bless me now, my Sa - vior, I come to Thee.

Text: Annie S. Hawks, 1835-1918
Tune: Robert Lowry, 1826-1899

Irregular
NEED
www.hymnary.org/text/i_need_thee_every_hour_most_graci_hawks

# December 27                               Expectations

*But without faith it is impossible to please Him, for he who comes
to God must believe that He is, and that He is a rewarder of those who
diligently seek Him.*                               Hebrews 11:6

We strive to believe with our whole heart that He is who He says He
is; that He is God Almighty. And if we earnestly seek Him, then He will
reward us, right? Yes, but...

Expectations. How they can trip us up in our walk. We can so easily
start to define what our lives should look like as He "rewards" us for our
faith and diligence. We begin to expect less stress, less pain, less illness,
less heartbreak, more answers to our prayers, even miraculous answers.
Surely our lives will just get rosier and rosier.

Ever so slowly, we begin to change our focus from Him and His
plans and purposes, to ourselves and our comfort and pleasure. We begin
to see any heartbreak in life as "undeserved"; any difficulty as
"unnecessary". We can be caught off guard.

How can we keep our hearts full of faith when the unexpected
shatters our world? In spite of any circumstance we face, we can choose
to "Be still, and know that I am God" (Psalm 46:10). Nothing takes Him
by surprise. Jesus tells us not to worry about our tomorrows (Matthew
6:34). All our futures are under His sovereign control and direction.

Psalm 118:24 directs: "This is the day the Lord has made; we will
rejoice and be glad in it." What we can know for sure is that we have been
given this moment, this day, to live. In childlike faith, we can choose to
walk joyfully through this day, hand in hand with Him, and leave all the
worries of our tomorrows in His loving and trustworthy care.

Let's come to Him with all the trust a child has in an all-wise Father.
Let's rejoice today, giving Him all our expectations for tomorrow, certain
that our prayers are being answered in His way, in His time and His plan.

**Today's Action:** Let's read Proverbs 27 together, welcoming its
reinforcement in wisdom for our lives.

*Do not boast about tomorrow, for you do not know
what a day may bring forth.*       *Proverbs 27:1*

# 'Tis So Sweet to Trust in Jesus

PROVERBS 30:5
Louisa M. R. Stead, 1882

William J. Kirkpatrick, 1882

1. 'Tis so sweet to trust in Je - sus, Just to take Him at His Word;
2. Oh, how sweet to trust in Je - sus, Just to trust His cleans - ing blood;
3. Yes, 'tis sweet to trust in Je - sus, Just from sin and self to cease;
4. I'm so glad I learned to trust Thee, Pre - cious Je - sus, Sav - ior, Friend;

Just to rest up - on His prom - ise, Just to know, "Thus saith the Lord!"
And in sim - ple faith to plunge me 'Neath the heal - ing, cleans - ing flood!
Just from Je - sus sim - ply tak - ing Life and rest, and joy and peace.
And I know that Thou art with me, Wilt be with me to the end.

*Refrain*

Je - sus, Je - sus, how I trust Him! How I've proved Him o'er and o'er;

Je - sus, Je - sus, pre - cious Je - sus! Oh, for grace to trust Him more!

# December 28                    Help My Unbelief

Does God heed our prayers if we have doubt? James says "But when you ask, you must believe and not doubt, because the one who doubts is like a wave of the sea, blown and tossed by the wind. That person should not expect to receive anything from the Lord." (James 1:6-7 NIV). It sure sounds like doubt would cause our prayers to go unheeded.

But does believing and not doubting mean having *no* doubt? Not likely. We probably will always have some lingering doubt. But we cannot ask in faith if we are *filled* with doubt.

In II Corinthians 5:7, we are told that "we walk by faith, not by sight." Walking by faith means we choose to believe, and then act on that belief in spite of our lingering doubt. We try to come to Him as unwaveringly as possible. And, just like a little child learning to walk, we can become more unwavering the more we practice "walking by faith".

Mark 9 tells us about the father who brought his demon-possessed child to Jesus. The father pleaded "But if You can do anything, have compassion on us and help us." He was not *filled* with faith. He didn't say "I *know* you can do anything!" He came with what little faith he had, asking with an "if". Jesus responded "All things are possible to him who believes." Mark reports that "Immediately the father of the child cried out and said with tears, 'Lord, I believe; help my unbelief!' " (Mark 9:24)

We can be so encouraged by this account. This father desired to believe with his whole heart. He had some faith, but he wasn't filled with faith. He knew he still had some unbelief. But he did not let his lingering doubt control him. He brought it to Jesus. What a perfect model for us.

Let's come wholeheartedly with what little faith we have, asking Him to deal with our remaining doubt. Let us take Him at His word, rest in His promises, and ask for grace to trust Him more.

**Today's Action**: Let's read Proverbs 28 together, choosing to place our trust in Him alone.

*Those who trust in the LORD will prosper;*
*those who trust in themselves are fools.*
Proverbs 28:25b, 26a NIV

# Am I a Soldier of the Cross

```
1. Am      I    a   sol - dier   of   the   cross,   A
2. Must    I   be  car - ried    to   the   skies    On
3. Are   there no foes   for     me   to   face?   Must
4. Sure    I  must fight  if      I  would reign;    In -
```

```
foll'- wer  of   the    Lamb?_  And  shall  I   fear   to
flow'- ry beds   of     ease,_  While o - thers fought to
I    not stem  the    flood?_  Is   this  vile world  a
crease my cour - age,   Lord!_  I'll  bear  the  toil,  en -
```

```
own   His cause,  Or   blush  to speak  His   name?
win   the prize,  And  sailed thro' bloo - dy   seas?
friend to grace,  To   help  me  on   to   God?
dure  the pain,  Sup - por - ted  by  Thy  Word.
```

Hymnary.org

# December 29           Take Courage

*For the eyes of the LORD run to and fro throughout the whole earth,*
*to show Himself strong on behalf of those whose heart is loyal to Him.*
                         II Chronicles 16:9

Isn't that an amazing image to ponder? The eyes of God Himself "run to and fro throughout the whole earth" looking for us; searching for us. Why? So He can strengthen us, so He can deliver us, so we can see Him at work. What an encouragement to stand firm in the faith. What a reason to take courage!

However, His deliverance is conditional. The verse just before this verse says "Because you relied on the LORD, He delivered" (II Chronicles 16:8). We must choose to fully rely on Him alone. He alone is able to deliver. He alone is worthy of trust. He alone is worthy of praise.

Let's ask Him to again examine our hearts and commit to rely fully on Him, to put our trust in Him alone. Then we can take courage. He will deliver. The victory is His, and therefore ours through our Lord Jesus!

But for those of us who may still be pretending and have not fully turned from our wickedness, today's Proverbs chapter begins with yet another stern warning – *Whoever remains stiff-necked after many rebukes will suddenly be destroyed – without remedy* (Proverbs 29:1 NIV). Let's be careful that we are not stiff-necked, refusing to repent, or we will suddenly be destroyed - without remedy. How tragic!

Let's thank and praise Him for His incredible promise that He searches us out in order to show Himself strong to us, so He can help us, so He can deliver us. Let's make sure our hearts are fully committed to Him as we ask Him to fill us with courage for the battle ahead.

**Today's Action:** Let's read Proverbs 29 together, committed to heeding its warnings so we can avoid the way of fools who are ensnared by sin. Instead, we are enabled to walk as the righteous ones, redeemed by Jesus, free to sing and be glad because of His great love for us.

*Evildoers are snared by their own sin, but the righteous*
*shout for joy and are glad.*       Proverbs 29:6 NIV

# Is Your All on the Altar?

ROMANS 12:1
E. A. H., 1900

Elisha A. Hoffman, 1900

1. You have longed for sweet peace, And for faith to in-crease, And have ear-nest-ly, fer-vent-ly prayed;
2. Would you walk with the Lord, In the light of His word, And have peace and con-tent-ment al - way?
3. Oh, we nev-er can know What the Lord will be-stow Of the bless-ings for which we have prayed;
4. Who can tell all the love He will send from a-bove, And how hap-py our hearts will be made;

But you can-not have rest, Or be per-fect-ly blest, Un-til all on the al-tar is laid.
You must do His sweet will, To be free from all ill, On the al-tar your all you must lay.
Till our bod-y and soul He doth ful-ly con-trol, And our all on the al-tar is laid.
Of the fel-low-ship sweet We shall share at His feet, When our all on the al-tar is laid.

*Refrain*

Is your all on the al-tar of sac-ri-fice laid? Your heart does the Spir-it con-trol?

You can on-ly be blest, And have peace and sweet rest, As you yield Him your bod-y and soul.

# December 30                                    Final Exam

*Since we are surrounded by so great a cloud of witnesses, let us lay aside*
*every weight, and the sin which so easily ensnares us, and let us run with*
*endurance the race that is set before us.*                    Hebrews 12:1

This is our last opportunity to examine our hearts before going into battle. If you have not turned from that sin He has been convicting you of, do it now. Before it's too late. Now. *Right now.*

We are not talking here about being sinless or perfect; none of us can be. But what we are dealing with is the attitude of our hearts. If we knowingly and rebelliously continue in sin, unwilling to fully repent and fully release it, then we would be well advised to lay down our weapons, step aside and not participate in this battle before us.

Let's face it. Your prayers will be hindered by your willful sin. Your sword won't be effective either if you are unwilling to allow your sword - His Word - to cut out that sin in your own life. You won't be able to expertly wield your weapons of warfare. You will be a laughing stock to our enemy. You risk being exposed for the hypocrite you are. You'd best excuse yourself before you are discovered and face expulsion.

Either choose a side, or step aside. We cannot fight with our whole heart if we have a divided heart. So let's get completely and fully right with God right now, or step aside.

Let's come before Almighty God, in humble submission to His kingship in our lives. Let's lay everything on the altar of sacrifice, and ask Him to reveal and strip away anything that may hinder our effectiveness in the battle ahead.

**Today's Action:** Let's read Proverbs 30 together. Let's allow ourselves to be filled with awe at the power of our Creator Commander, and submit ourselves to His fitting us for battle, even if that includes stripping away that easily ensnaring "secret" sin.

*There are those who are clean in their own eyes*
*but are not washed of their filth.*
Proverbs 30:12 ESV

# To God Be the Glory (Crosby)

GALATIANS 1:4-5
Frances J. Crosby, pub. 1875

William H. Doane, pub. 1875

1. To God be the glo - ry, great things He hath done, So loved He the world that He gave us His Son,
2. Oh, per - fect re - demp - tion, the pur - chase of blood, To eve - ry be - liev - er the prom - ise of God;
3. Great things He hath taught us, great things He hath done, And great our re - joic - ing through Je - sus the Son;

Who yield - ed His life an a - tone - ment for sin, And o - pened the life gate that all may go in.
The vil - est of - fen - der who tru - ly be - lieves, That mo - ment from Je - sus a par - don re - ceives.
But pur - er, and high - er, and great - er will be Our won - der, our trans - port, when Je - sus we see.

*Refrain*

Praise the Lord, praise the Lord, let the earth hear His voice! Praise the Lord, praise the Lord, Let the peo - ple re - joice!

Oh, come to the Fa - ther, through Je - sus the Son, And give Him the glo - ry, great things He hath done.

*Hymnary.org*

# December 31                    The Roar of the Father

*I looked for someone among them who would build up the wall and
stand before Me in the gap on behalf of the land so I would not have to
destroy it, but I found no one.*                    Ezekiel 22:30 NIV

The God of the universe is looking for intercessors to stand in the gap
on behalf of our land so He won't have to destroy it. He sees us. We have
answered the call and completed 30 days of preparation. But maybe we
are skeptical and think, "What difference can our prayers really make?"

Bible teacher Priscilla Shirer[11] recounts a scene from *The Lion King*.[12]
Little Simba is in trouble because he disobeyed his father's command. His
life is now threatened by the hyaenas. He tries his best to roar, but all that
comes out sounds more like a whimper. The hyaenas mock him: "Is that
the best you got?" As Simba tries again, from behind him comes the roar
of his father, Mufasa. Mufasa's powerful roar fills the cave and
echoes down the canyon walls, scattering the hyaenas in fear. That's the
roar of the father. That's the roar of our Father.

May that image fill our hearts with courage as we engage in this fight.
We know that, in answer to our desperate, fervent, albeit whimpered
cries, our Father, the Creator, the Lord of Hosts, God Almighty, will
come with His roar to scatter the enemy, and accomplish His will.

God promises "Call upon Me in the day of trouble; I will deliver you,
and you shall glorify Me" (Psalm 50:15). As His people, we are answering
His call to stand in the gap on behalf of our land and open our mouths
on behalf of those who cannot, or will not, speak for themselves.

Will our prayers be heard? Absolutely! Will we see the evidence? Not
necessarily. But since we walk by faith, not by sight (II Corinthians 5:7),
we know the victory has already been won. He has called us to pray, and
we obey. The battle belongs to the Lord. May we be His faithful warriors.

**Today's Action:** Let's read Proverbs 31 together and commit to
applying its instruction to our lives.

*Open your mouth for the speechless, in the cause
of all who are appointed to die.*       Proverbs 31:8

# 6

# THE FINAL PREPARATION

*So He said to them, "This kind can come out by nothing but prayer and fasting."*                    Mark 9:29

## New Year's Day – Call to Prayer and Fasting

A call has gone out for a time of prayer and fasting on New Year's Day, January 1. Why has this call been issued?

Prayer is often accompanied by fasting in the Bible. As esteemed theologian, Wayne Grudem, writes, "Fasting expresses earnestness and urgency in our prayers; if we continued to fast, eventually we would die. Therefore, in a symbolic way, fasting says to God that we are prepared to lay down our lives that the situation be changed rather than that it continue."[13]

Prayer with fasting acknowledges that we are truly in dire straits. This is urgent business. The future of our nation may depend on it. The safety of our children may depend on it. The protection of religious liberty and our freedom to worship God may depend on it. The spread of Christianity around the world may depend on it. Who knows if we have not been called together to pray "for such a time as this" (Esther 4:14)?

Another reason to call for a time of fasting and prayer is that Jesus taught that some spiritual battles are so serious, they can only be dealt with through prayer and fasting (Matthew 17:21; Mark 9:29). If we see this time as so pivotal in our nation's history, wouldn't it make sense to pull out all the stops, to do whatever we could to ensure the best possible outcome?

If we answer this call to pray and fast on New Year's Day, what might this look like in each of our individual life situations? That is a question that can only be answered by each of us individually seeking the Lord for ourselves. Some of us may be able to lead our entire family in a day of prayer and fasting, demonstrating how historical and critical this moment is. Some of us may be led to just take in liquid all day, fasting from solid food. Others may only be able to skip a meal or two because of the obligations we have. Yet others of us may have medical issues so we are not able to go without food, not even for a single meal. But everyone can give up something – second servings? dessert? Let's just not let this become legalistic. Let's each simply ask the Lord what He would have us do in obedience to this call to fast and pray.

More importantly than *what* we choose as a fast is *why* we choose to fast. If our motive is to be seen by others as more righteous, then our actions will not be blessed. Jesus instructs in Matthew 6:1 (NIV) "Be careful not to practice your righteousness in front of others to be seen by them. If you do, you will have no reward from your Father in heaven." He then further instructs "When you fast, do not look somber as the hypocrites do, for they disfigure their faces to show others they are fasting. Truly I tell you, they have received their reward in full" (Matthew 6:16 NIV).

Jesus goes on to tell us the proper attitude in fasting: "But when you fast, put oil on your head and wash your face, so that it will not be obvious to others that you are fasting, but only to your Father, who is unseen; and your Father, who sees what is done in secret, will reward you" (Matthew 6:17-18 NIV).

Jesus did not say "*If* you fast..." He said "*When* you fast..." The assumption is that we will fast from time to time. But Jesus tells us to do it in such a way that it does not call attention to ourselves for the purpose of people's praise, but only to be seen by God Himself.

People judge by outward appearances; God looks at and judges our hearts (I Samuel 16:7). He is the only One whose praise we seek as we make a plan for New Year's Day. As He leads, we choose to set aside some portion or all of this day in fasting and prayer in advance of our momentous, coordinated attack on our enemy and his demonic forces.

Throughout this New Year's Day, as we focus our hearts and minds on our 50-day prayer challenge ahead, let's ask the Lord what He would like to accomplish through our prayers. What changes in the hearts and lives of us, His people, would be pleasing to Him? What areas of concern would He like us to bring to Him in prayer? And what would He like to see accomplished in the heart and life of our nation as a whole?

As we seek His face and listen to His direction, we may want to use the following space to record the specific concerns He brings to mind. Then we can refer to this list during our 50 days of intercession and be reminded of His heart for us and our country.

Notes for Intercession:

_____

_____

_____

_____

_____

_____

_____

_____

# 7

# SHOULDER TO SHOULDER

*I looked for someone among them who would build up the wall and stand before Me in the gap on behalf of the land so I would not have to destroy it, but I found no one.* Ezekiel 22:30 NIV

## 50 Days of Intercession

The final phase of this prayer project consists of 50 days of intercessory prayer. This part of the program begins January 2 and ends February 20. We come together as brothers and sisters in the Lord from all 50 States. Shoulder to shoulder, we stand before the Lord in the gap on behalf of ourselves, our brothers and sisters in Christ, and our nation.

The book of Psalms will serve as our framework during these 50 days of prayer. Psalms is a book of praise and petition to the Lord. The Psalms remind us to "Be still and know that I am God" (Psalm 46:10). They remind us that God alone is our refuge and strength (Psalm 46:1); He alone is our rock and our salvation (Psalm 62:2); He alone is our shelter in times of trouble (Psalm 27:5 NIV). The Psalms also lead us in praise to Him for answering when we cry out to Him in repentance and dependence (Psalm 34:6).

We have divided the book of Psalms into 50 daily Psalm Reading (PR) sections. Each State has been assigned its own section to start with on January 2 and then continue to rotate through the next sections of the Psalms each day. In this way, the entire book of Psalms will be lifted to the Lord for 50 days, with rotating sections being read by prayer warriors from each State. Additionally, each prayer warrior will have read through the entire book of Psalms in 50 days, with each section taking only 5-7 minutes of reading per day.

Each State will begin with the Psalm Reading (PR) section that matches that State's alphabetical rank when listed alphabetically among the 50 States. For example, Alabama is the first State when listed alphabetically. Therefore, on January 2nd, our first day of prayer, intercessors in Alabama will begin with Psalm Reading 1 (PR 1). But on that same day, Californians will begin with Psalm Reading 5 (PR 5) because California is the 5th of the 50 States alphabetically. Texans will begin with Psalm Reading 43 since Texas is the 43rd State in the alphabetical list of States. Each State then rotates daily through each of the 50 Psalm Reading sections.

An alphabetical listing of States, along with the first reading assignment, is provided on pages 88 and 89. Once you have identified what Psalm Reading (PR) section you will be starting with on our first day of prayer, you can simply write "Jan 2" on the line next to your State's assignment and then fill in the subsequent dates for the remaining 49 divisions through February 20.

For intercessors in the District of Columbia as well as various U. S. Territories, you can line up with any State that you prefer, or you can start by reading PR 1 with Alabama. However, since Wyoming is both the last and the least populated State, you may wish to join with them. Wyoming is the 50th State, so Wyoming intercessors will be starting with Psalm

Reading 50 (PR 50) on January 2nd, moving to Psalm Reading 1 (PR 1) on January 3rd, and continue daily rotating through the sections, ending with Psalm Reading 49 (PR 49) on the last day, February 20.

Our first day of prayer will begin with our assigned Psalm reading based on our State of residence, and each subsequent day will rotate through each of the 50 portions of Psalms. Even when read aloud, each Psalm reading will typically take an average of 5-7 minutes per day. This means that each of us as intercessors, spending around 5-7 minutes per day, will have read every word of the book of Psalms by the end of this 50-day period as we rotate progressively through each of the 50 Psalm readings.

As we read our respective Psalm reading selection for each day, let's ask the Lord to lead us in what He would like us to bring before Him in prayer that day. The subjects may change from day to day based on the Psalm reading selection for that day. Or some of us may have a particular burden on our hearts that will be the same throughout several or all of the 50 days. Let's simply ask Him to guide us in what He wants us to bring to Him in prayer.

The plan is simple:

1.  Find your State's ranking when listed alphabetically. The list is on pages 88-89.
2.  Start your first day of prayer, January 2, with the Psalm reading assignment that corresponds to your State's ranking.
3.  Proceed chronologically through the rest of the 50 Psalm reading sections daily, reading the last remaining section on February 20.
4.  Daily devotions and hymns are provided to accompany each of the Psalm reading sections. These hymns and devotions are intended to encourage and embolden us as we read our Psalms to the Lord and then engage in intercession. Begin with the devotion that corresponds to your State's alphabetical position number, then continue to rotate daily through all 50 devotions and Psalm readings. Following this pattern, the entire book of Psalms will have been lifted to the Lord each and every day for 50 days by prayer warriors from all 50 States.

Let's keep in mind that the purpose of these 50 days of dedicated prayer is to stand in the gap for our fellow Christians and for our nation as a whole. Let's ask the Lord to purify the hearts and lives of His people, returning us to our "first love" (Revelation 2:4). Let's pray that He will enable us, His people, to turn from our wicked ways, so that He, Almighty God, will forgive our sins and heal our land (II Chronicles 7:14).

Let us together rejoice that He has called each one of us to the privilege of interceding at this time for His purposes to be accomplished in our lives and in the life of our nation. Let's prepare to engage, shoulder to shoulder, faithfully standing in the gap for our land!

We have submitted ourselves to Him during the 31 Days of Preparation so He can cleanse us and equip us to become powerful intercessors in this spiritual battle. Let's now engage the enemy and take back the territory that has been surrendered!

Because of Jesus, our victory is assured! Our faithful fighting is all that remains to be done. As we cry out to Him over the next 50 days, He will hear our whole-hearted, desperate cries and empower them for the tearing down of strongholds, for the restoration of the hearts of His people and for the healing of our nation.

May our nation be renewed as the beacon of hope and the bright light that it once was for His kingdom, and for the spreading of the gospel of good news to all the world.

Let the battle begin.

# I AM A DISCIPLE

The die has been cast.
I have stepped over the line.
The decision has been made.
I AM A DISCIPLE OF JESUS CHRIST.

I will not look back,
   let up,
   slow down,
   back away,
   or be still.

I no longer need preeminence,
   prosperity,
   position,
   promotions,
   praises,
   or popularity.

I do not have to be right,
   first,
   tops,
   recognized,
   regarded,
   or rewarded.

I now live by faith,
   love by patience,
   lift by prayer,
   and labor by power.

My pace is set.
My gait is fast.
My goal is heaven.
My road is narrow.
My way is rough.
My companions few.
My Guide is reliable.
My mission is clear.

I cannot be bought,
   compromised,
   deterred,
   lured away,
   turned back,
   diluted,
   or delayed.

I will not flinch in the face of
sacrifice, hesitate in the presence
of adversity, negotiate at the
table of the enemy, pander at the
pool of popularity, nor meander
in the maze of mediocrity.

I will not give up,
   back up,
   let up,
   or shut up
   until I have prayed up,
   preached up,
   stored up and stayed up
   for the cause of Christ.
I AM A DISCIPLE OF JESUS CHRIST.

I must go 'til He returns,
   give until I drop,
   preach until all know,
   and work until He stops me.

And when He comes to get
His own, He will have no
trouble recognizing me.

My colors are flying high,
and they are clear for all to see.
I AM A DISCIPLE OF JESUS CHRIST.

In the face of death, this was written by an African man martyred in the 1800's. Often called *I Am a Disciple,* it is also known as *The Creed of the Fellowship of the Unashamed.* "For I am not ashamed of the Gospel, because it is the power of God for the salvation of everyone who believes."  Romans 1:16

# 50 Psalm Readings

| State | ✓ | Date | Psalm Reading Divisions |
|---|---|---|---|
| 1. ALABAMA | ☐ | _____ | **PR 1:** Psalms 1 – 5 |
| 2. ALASKA | ☐ | _____ | **PR 2:** Psalms 6 – 9 |
| 3. ARIZONA | ☐ | _____ | **PR 3:** Psalms 10 – 14 |
| 4. ARKANSAS | ☐ | _____ | **PR 4:** Psalms 15-17, 19 |
| 5. CALIFORNIA | ☐ | _____ | **PR 5:** Psalms 18, 20 |
| 6. COLORADO | ☐ | _____ | **PR 6:** Psalms 21 – 23 |
| 7. CONNECTICUT | ☐ | _____ | **PR 7:** Psalms 24 – 27 |
| 8. DELAWARE | ☐ | _____ | **PR 8:** Psalms 28 – 31 |
| 9. FLORIDA | ☐ | _____ | **PR 9:** Psalms 32 – 34 |
| 10. GEORGIA | ☐ | _____ | **PR 10:** Psalms 35, 38 |
| 11. HAWAII | ☐ | _____ | **PR 11:** Psalms 36 & 37 |
| 12. IDAHO | ☐ | _____ | **PR 12:** Psalms 39 – 41 |
| 13. ILLINOIS | ☐ | _____ | **PR 13:** Psalms 42 – 45 |
| 14. INDIANA | ☐ | _____ | **PR 14:** Psalms 46 – 49 |
| 15. IOWA | ☐ | _____ | **PR 15:** Psalms 50 – 52 |
| 16. KANSAS | ☐ | _____ | **PR 16:** Psalms 53 – 56 |
| 17. KENTUCKY | ☐ | _____ | **PR 17:** Psalms 57 – 59 |
| 18. LOUISIANA | ☐ | _____ | **PR 18:** Psalms 60 – 63 |
| 19. MAINE | ☐ | _____ | **PR 19:** Psalms 64 – 66 |
| 20. MARYLAND | ☐ | _____ | **PR 20:** Psalms 67 & 68 |
| 21. MASSACHUSETTS | ☐ | _____ | **PR 21:** Psalms 69 & 70 |
| 22. MICHIGAN | ☐ | _____ | **PR 22:** Psalms 71 & 72 |
| 23. MINNESOTA | ☐ | _____ | **PR 23:** Psalms 73 & 74 |
| 24. MISSISSIPPI | ☐ | _____ | **PR 24:** Psalms 75 – 77 |
| 25. MISSOURI | ☐ | _____ | **PR 25:** Psalm 78 |

| State | ✓ | Date | Psalm Reading Divisions |
|-------|---|------|-------------------------|
| 26. MONTANA | ☐ | _____ | **PR 26:** Psalms 79 – 81 |
| 27. NEBRASKA | ☐ | _____ | **PR 27:** Psalms 82 – 85 |
| 28. NEVADA | ☐ | _____ | **PR 28:** Psalms 86 – 88 |
| 29. NEW HAMPSHIRE | ☐ | _____ | **PR 29:** Psalm 89 |
| 30. NEW JERSEY | ☐ | _____ | **PR 30:** Psalms 90 – 92 |
| 31. NEW MEXICO | ☐ | _____ | **PR 31:** Psalms 93 – 96 |
| 32. NEW YORK | ☐ | _____ | **PR 32:** Psalms 97 – 101 |
| 33. NORTH CAROLINA | ☐ | _____ | **PR 33:** Psalms 102 & 103 |
| 34. NORTH DAKOTA | ☐ | _____ | **PR 34:** Psalms 104, 108 |
| 35. OHIO | ☐ | _____ | **PR 35:** Psalm 105 |
| 36. OKLAHOMA | ☐ | _____ | **PR 36:** Psalm 106 |
| 37. OREGON | ☐ | _____ | **PR 37:** Psalms 107, 110 |
| 38. PENNSYLVANIA | ☐ | _____ | **PR 38:** Psalms 109, 111-112 |
| 39. RHODE ISLAND | ☐ | _____ | **PR 39:** Psalms 113 – 115 |
| 40. SOUTH CAROLINA | ☐ | _____ | **PR 40:** Psalms 116 - 118 |
| 41. SOUTH DAKOTA | ☐ | _____ | **PR 41:** Psalm 119: 1-56 |
| 42. TENNESSEE | ☐ | _____ | **PR 42:** Psalm 119: 57-112 |
| 43. TEXAS | ☐ | _____ | **PR 43:** Psalm 119: 113-176 |
| 44. UTAH | ☐ | _____ | **PR 44:** Psalms 120 – 126 |
| 45. VERMONT | ☐ | _____ | **PR 45:** Psalms 127 – 132 |
| 46. VIRGINIA | ☐ | _____ | **PR 46:** Psalms 133-5, 137, 138 |
| 47. WASHINGTON | ☐ | _____ | **PR 47:** Psalms 136, 139 |
| 48. WEST VIRGINIA | ☐ | _____ | **PR 48:** Psalms 140 – 143 |
| 49. WISCONSIN | ☐ | _____ | **PR 49:** Psalms 144 – 146 |
| 50. WYOMING | ☐ | _____ | **PR 50:** Psalms 147 – 150 |

# O Jesus, I Have Promised

Words: John E. Bode
Music: Arthur H. Mann

# Reading 1: Psalms 1-5 Why?

*The kings of the earth rise up and the rulers band together against the LORD and against His anointed, saying, "Let us break Their chains and throw off Their shackles."* Psalm 2:2-3 NIV

When we look around, we often wonder "Why can't we just all get along?" Why is there such division, anger and hatred among nations, in communities, even in families? In particular, why is there persecution and martyrdom? Why will some people kill others simply because of their beliefs?

Psalm 2 explains it. Christians choose to live by God's moral standard as outlined in His Holy Word. We seek to please Him because He gave His life to redeem us. But unbelievers see God's moral standard as simply constraints designed to spoil their fun. They think no one and nothing should get in the way of their pleasure. The goal of their rebellious, "enlightened" spirits is to break free from God's "chains" and throw off His "shackles". This often includes punishing or eliminating those who stand up to their rebellion against God, who dare call their rebellion "sin".

Such was the case of the young minister martyred in Africa for his faith centuries ago. In reading his declaration on page 87, you can feel his determination, his will to stand firm in his faith. This infuriated his opponents all the more, to the point of killing him. But he knew that, no matter what they did, his past was redeemed; his future secure. He had nothing to fear, not even death.

As we intercede for each other and our nation, may we be encouraged by his words as they ring through the centuries. No matter what may come, may we boldly declare "I am a disciple of Jesus Christ." With Paul, may we firmly say, "I am not ashamed of the Gospel of Christ, for it is the power of God to salvation for everyone who believes" (Romans 1:16).

And when He comes to claim His own, may He have no trouble recognizing us. May our colors fly high for all to see that we, too, are disciples of Jesus Christ.

# This Is My Father's World

Words: Maltbie D. Babcock
Music: Traditional English Melody; Arrangement: S. F. L.

# Reading 2: Psalms 6-9                    What is Man?

*What is man that You are mindful of him?*   Psalm 8:4

As a shepherd by trade, David likely spent many a dark night out with his sheep. One can imagine that he often "considered" the heavens, as he writes in Psalm 8. Observing the immensity of the universe, he marvels "What is man that You are mindful of him?" (Psalm 8:4)

If we contemplate the complexity of His creation, we too will marvel that He cares for each of us individually. If we try to wrap our minds around the fact that every hair on our head is numbered (Luke 12:7) and that He is "intimately acquainted" with all our ways (Psalm 139:3 AMP), it is too much for us to grasp.

Not only does He know all things about each of us, but He also cares about, and is involved in, the details of our lives. In Psalm 9, David reminds us that our God is a refuge for the oppressed, a defense in times of trouble, and that He will not forsake those who seek Him and place their trust in Him (Psalm 9:9-10). What comfort.

David also knew that sometimes we need times of trouble in order to recognize our need for the Lord. He petitions, "Put them in fear, O LORD, that the nations may know themselves to be but men" (Psalm 9:20).

This is an appropriate prayer for us to pray today, not only over our nation and our world, but over each one of us individually. Together, let's ask Him to put us all in an appropriate awe and fear of Him, so we see ourselves to be "but men". Only He can quicken our consciences, convicting us of our sin.

May we all ask Him for His reality check, so we will see who we truly are - just sinful people in need of our Savior. Whether it is a need to repent and turn from sin, or a need for wisdom and provision to get through the next 24 hours, we all need Jesus.

# We Have An Anchor

1. Will your an - chor hold in the storms of life, When the
2. It is safe - ly moored, 'twill the storm with - stand, For 'tis
3. When our eyes be - hold thru the gath - 'ring night The

clouds un - fold their wings of strife? When the strong tides lift,
well se - cured by the Sav - ior's hand; And the ca - bles passed
cit - y of gold, our har - bor bright, We shall an - chor fast

and the ca - bles strain, Will your an - chor drift, or firm re - main?
from His heart to mine, Can de - fy the blast, thru strength di - vine.
by the heav'n - ly shore, With the storms all past for - ev - er - more.

**Chorus**

We have an an - chor that keeps the soul Stead - fast and sure while the bil - lows roll,

Fas - tened to the Rock which can - not move, Ground - ed firm and deep in the Sav - ior's love.

Words: Priscilla J. Owens
Music: William J. Kirkpatrick

# Reading 3: Psalms 10-14                    Wise or a Fool?

*The fool says in his heart, "There is no God."*    Psalm 14:1 ESV

Today's Psalms spend much time describing the fool. In arrogance and pride, the fool says "There is no God; He will never see" (Psalm 14:1; Psalm 10:11). As a result, they boast of the cravings of their heart and boldly renounce God's principles; they celebrate wickedness, are corrupt, murder the innocent, and do "abominable works" (Psalms 10:3, 8; 12:8; and 14:1). Doesn't that describe much of our world today?

No one likes to be considered the fool. We tend to equate a fool with one who is ignorant and lacks intelligence. But taken in context, the Hebrew word translated here as "fool" refers to someone devoid of moral character, rather than someone lacking intelligence.

Many highly intelligent people deny the reality of God's existence. Why? It's not because of ignorance. Instead, it's more likely an issue of arrogance. They think "No one's going to tell me what I can and can't do!" Tossing out God's moral compass, they choose to do whatever they please, whenever they please. They live for the moment, ignoring the reality of eternal consequences. Fools, indeed.

Jesus repeats this same thought in His parable of the wise and foolish builder. The wise man listened and built his life on the Word. When the storms of life hit, his house stood firm. However, the foolish man ignored the rock-solid foundation of God's ways, and built his house on sand instead. When faced with the realities of life, Jesus said "great was its fall" (Matthew 7:27).

Let's ask the Lord today to show us if there are areas in our lives where we are not lining up with the building code of His Word. Let's be wise and anchor our lives on the solid rock of His truth. Let's intercede for those who have been blinded by the deceptions of the enemy. May they be given sight and see their need to build their lives in keeping with His ways.

# O That Will Be Glory

Charles Hutchinson Gabriel, 1900

Charles Hutchinson Gabriel

1. When all my la-bors and tri-als are o'er, And I am safe on that beau-ti-ful shore, Just to be near the dear Lord I a-dore, Will through the ag-es be glo-ry for me.

2. When, by the gift of His in-fi-nite grace, I am ac-cord-ed in hea-ven a place, Just to be there and to look on His face, Will through the ag-es be glo-ry for me.

3. Friends will be there I have loved long a-go; Joy like a ri-ver a-round me will flow; Yet just a smile from my Sav-ior, I know, Will through the ag-es be glo-ry for me.

*Refrain*

O that will be glo-ry for me, Glo-ry for me, glo-ry for me, When by His grace I shall look on His face, That will be glo-ry, be glo-ry for me.

# Reading 4: Psalms 15-17, 19            Eternity

*In Your presence is fullness of joy.* Psalm 16:11

In today's Psalms, David expresses grave concern for his life. But then he moves his focus from the difficulties of this temporal, earthly experience to the permanence of the eternal. "As for me", he says, "I shall be satisfied when I awake in Your likeness" (Psalm 17:15).

When we turn our eyes from this world to the next, what a beautiful place to find rest for our souls. There are so many things beyond our control in this short experience we call life. Right now, it may seem like our difficulties will last forever. But this life will be over before we know it. Then we will experience fullness of joy in His presence forever.

Fullness of joy! We can't even begin to comprehend what that would be like. In perfected bodies, there will be no more pain, no sickness, no sorrow; no more stresses, no anxiety, no uncertainty. It's hard to imagine a life like that, for all eternity! But what we do know is that it will be even more amazing than we can begin to imagine. "Beloved, it has not yet been revealed what we shall be, but we know that when He is revealed, we shall be like Him, for we shall see Him as He is" (I John 3:2).

May our hearts be filled with the wonder of it all - that He would love us so much that He would come and live a perfect life and die such a horrific death in order for us to be with Him for all eternity. Such love! Such joy! Such hope!

As we read these Psalms and intercede on behalf of each other and our nation, may we be energized with certainty today. Regardless of the circumstances we face, they cannot impact our eternal destiny. In the twinkling of an eye, we will all be changed (I Corinthians 15:52). So let's keep our eye on the eternal and, in what will seem like just a blink, we will be with Him for all eternity.

# Trusting Jesus

1. Sim - ply trus - ting ev' - ry day, Trus - ting thro' a stor - my way;
2. Bright - ly does His Spi - rit shine In - to this poor heart__ of mine;
3. Sing - ing if my way is clear, Pra - ying if the path__ be drear;
4. Trus - ting Him while life shall last, Trus - ting Him till earth__ be past;

E - ven when my faith is small, Trus - ting Je - sus, that is all.
While He leads I can - not fall; Trus - ting Je - sus, that is all.
If in dan - ger for Him call; Trus - ting Je - sus, that is all.
Till with - in the jas - per wall, Trus - ting Je - sus, that is all.

Trus - ting as the mo - ments fly, Trus - ting as the days go by;

Trus - ting him what - e'er be - fall, Trus - ting Je - sus, that is all.

Text: Edgar Page Stites, 1836-1912
Tune: Ira D. Sankey, 1840-1908

77 77 Refrain
TRUSTING JESUS
www.hymnary.org/text/simply_trusting_every_day

# Reading 5: Psalms 18, 20                    Fighting Fear

*Some trust in chariots and some in horses, but*
*we trust in the name of the LORD our God.* Psalm 20:7 ESV

Psalm 18 is David's song of deliverance after God saved him from King Saul and his army. David was being hunted by the king himself and his military forces. But David chose to trust in the Lord, and God rescued him in a mighty way.

David describes the awesome power God displayed in His rescue: the earth trembled, the mountains shook; He bowed the heavens and flew upon the wings of the wind; His voice thundered from the heavens; He sent out hailstones and fire; He sent His arrows and lightning, scattering and vanquishing the enemy (Psalm 18:7-14).

Our mighty God rules the heavens and the earth. But David also knows He is attentive to the cries and heartaches of each one of His children. He knows our troubles, our burdens, and He knows our fears.

What is fear? It is an effective tool of our enemy. What makes fear one of his most powerful weapons against our faith? It's because it is rooted in distrust. When there is uncertainty in our lives, fear makes it hard to choose to simply trust God. We want to be in control; we want to fix it. Our focus is in an inappropriate place, because our eyes are locked in on ourselves and our circumstances. But there is no help to be found there. Our help only comes from the Lord, the maker of heaven and earth (Psalm 121:2).

We join forces together in prayer today because we can trust our Almighty God to deliver us. We choose to trust Him in every circumstance and bring Him every fear. We choose to take "every thought into captivity to the obedience of Christ" (II Corinthians 10:5), by speaking truth to those fearful emotions our enemy tries to plant in our minds. Instead, we place our trust in the name of Him who alone is our strength, our rock, our fortress, our deliverer, our shield, our stronghold and our salvation.

# Jesus Shall Reign

1. Je - sus shall reign wher - e'er the sun Does its suc -
2. To Him shall end - less pray'r be made, And end - less
3. Peo - ple and realms of ev' - ry tongue Dwell on His
4. Let ev' - ry crea - ture rise and bring Ho - nor and

ces - sive jour - neys run; His king - dom spread from
prai - ses crown His head; His name like sweet per -
love with sweet - est song, And in - fant voi - ces
glo - ry to our King; An - gels des - cend with

shore to shore, Till moons shall wax and wane no more.
fume shall rise With ev' - ry mor - ning sac - ri - fice.
shall pro - claim Their ear - ly bles - sings on His name.
songs a - gain, And earth re - peat the loud "A - men"!

Text: Isaac Watts, 1674-1748
Tune: John Hatton, c. 1710-1793

88 88
DUKE STREET
www.hymnary.org/text/jesus_shall_reign_wherever_the_sun

# Reading 6: Psalms 21-23                    Prophecy

*All the ends of the world shall remember and turn to the LORD...*
                                                    Psalm 22:27a

T oday's Psalm reading includes the familiar 23rd Psalm: "The LORD is my shepherd; I shall not want." What comfort is found in these words: "Yea, though I walk through the valley of the shadow of death, I will fear no evil, for You are with me" (Psalm 23:1).

Today's Psalm reading also includes very specific details about Jesus' death, written nearly 1,000 years before they actually took place: "All those who see Me ridicule Me; they hurl insults; they shake the head, saying, "He trusted in the LORD; let Him rescue Him.' A band of evil men has encircled Me, they pierced My hands and My feet; they divide My garments among them and for My clothing they cast lots" (Psalm 22:7-8; 16; 18).

After His resurrection, Jesus explained to His disciples why He had to die: " 'This is what I told you while I was still with you: everything must be fulfilled that is written about Me in the Law of Moses, the Prophets and the Psalms' " (Luke 24:44). How amazing that God Himself, in the person of Jesus Christ, validated the Old Testament in this way, including the Book of Psalms.

Toward the end of Psalm 22, there is prophecy that may be in the process of reaching fulfillment: "All the ends of the world shall remember and turn to the LORD" (Psalm 22:27). Is it possible that part of the Lord's purpose in calling us to prayer at this time is to usher in the completion of this final prophecy?

May we be strengthened and emboldened as we read Psalms 21-23 to Him today and intercede for each other and our world. Let's pray that now would be the completion of the prophecy that all the ends of the earth will remember and turn to the Lord, including prodigals from every nation, tribe and tongue, "for dominion belongs to the LORD and He rules over the nations" (Psalm 22:28 NIV).

# A Wonderful Savior

1. A wonderful Savior is Jesus my Lord, A wonderful Savior to me; He hideth my soul in the cleft of the rock, Where rivers of pleasure I see.

2. A wonderful Savior is Jesus my Lord, He taketh my burden away, He holdeth me up, and I shall not be moved, He giveth me strength as my day.

3. When clothed in His brightness, transported I rise To meet Him in clouds of the sky, His perfect salvation, His wonderful love, I'll shout with the millions on high.

*Chorus*

He hideth my soul in the cleft of the rock That shadows a dry, thirsty land; He hideth my life in the depths of His love, And covers me there with His hand, And covers me there with His hand.

Words by Fanny J. Crosby
Music by William J. Kirkpatrick

PDHymns.com

# Reading 7: Psalms 24-27        A Greater Fear

*The LORD is my light and my salvation; whom shall I fear?*
Psalm 27:1a

Many Psalms were written when David was in real fear. His very life was often threatened, first by King Saul and later even by his own son, Absalom. Fear can be a significant factor in all of our lives from time to time.

But fear can be a useful tool. It can help us realize our helplessness in and of ourselves. But also, a greater fear can overcome or cast out a lesser fear. By having a *greater fear* (respect or awe) for the God who preserves and protects, David could let go of his *lesser fear* of what man might do to him. Instead, he could choose to put his trust in God. David recognized that "The LORD is the strength of my life;" which allowed him to say, "of whom shall I be afraid" (Psalm 27:1b)?

A healthy fear of God's justice can also be very useful. An appropriate fear of God can keep us from sinning. Moses told the Israelites, "Do not fear; for God has come to test you, and that His fear may be before you, so that you may not sin" (Exodus 20:20).

As people, we will always worship something – either God or ourselves. Our natural tendency is to please ourselves – always being concerned with self. Self *-ish*. We are called to be self – *less*; to die to self through the substitutionary death of Jesus, who died in our place.

As we read Psalms 24-27 to the Lord today, let us be comforted that "The earth is the LORD's, and everything in it" (Psalm 24:1 NIV). He is, and always will be, on His Throne. Nothing that happens is a surprise to Him. As we come before Him in prayer, let's ask Him to use our fears to bring all of us to the end of ourselves, to turn us away from our sin, and draw us back to Himself. Then we can all face our futures without fear.

# Moment By Moment

1. Dy - ing with Je - sus, by death reck-oned mine; Liv-ing with Je - sus, a
2. Nev - er a tri - al that He is not there, Nev - er a bur - den that
3. Nev - er a heart-ache, and nev - er a groan, Nev - er a tear - drop and
4. Nev - er a weak - ness that He doth not feel, Nev - er a sick - ness that

new life di - vine; Look-ing to Je - sus till glo - ry doth shine, Mo-ment by
He doth not bear, Nev - er a sor - row that He doth not share, Mo-ment by
nev - er a moan; Nev - er a dan - ger but there on the throne, Mo-ment by
He can - not heal; Mo - ment by mo-ment, in woe or in weal, Je - sus my

*Fine* *Chorus*

mo - ment, O Lord, I am Thine.
mo - ment, I'm un - der His care. Mo-ment by mo-ment I'm kept in His love; Mo-ment by
mo - ment He thinks of His own.
Sav - ior, a - bides with me still.

*D.S.*— mo - ment, O Lord, I am Thine.

*D.S. al Fine*

mo - ment I've life from a - bove; Look-ing to Je - sus till glo - ry doth shine; Mo-ment by

Words by Maj. D. W. Whittle
Music by May Whittle Moody

*PDHymns.com*

# Reading 8: Psalms 28-31                    In His Hands

*You are my God. My times are in Your hand.* Psalm 31:14b-15a

In these Psalms, David not only powerfully reminds us of who our God is, but also why He alone can be trusted with the concerns of our lives: God alone "sat enthroned at the Flood; and the LORD sits as King forever" (Psalm 29:10).

David leads by example in choosing to trust, in choosing to put his hope in God alone. David tells us "But as for me, I will trust in You, O LORD; I say 'You are my God.' My times are in Your hand" (Psalm 31:14-15). What a place of peace and refuge, a place of trust and rest. Regardless of how uncertain or difficult our circumstances are or may become, we can choose to trust Him as we remind ourselves of this truth: Our times are in His hands.

David ends today's reading with this encouragement: "Be strong and take heart, all you who hope in the LORD" (Psalm 31:24 NIV). So let us choose to put our hope in the LORD. Then we can be of good courage, because He promises to strengthen us.

The best way to allow Him to strengthen our hearts is to immerse ourselves in His Word. The truth that He works all things together for the good of those who love Him (Romans 8:28) is a wonderful truth to encourage our trust. The fact that He has gone to prepare a place for us (John 14:2) is another reason for hope. The promise that nothing can separate us from His love (Romans 8:38-39) and that He is with us even to the end of the world (Matthew 28:20) are even more reasons to have hope and not be afraid.

As we read these Psalms to Him, let's remember these truths: He is sovereign. He is enthroned as King forever. And He is working out His will, in His way, and in His time. May He direct us and fill us with courage as we engage in battle today.

# The Solid Rock

Text: Edward Mote, 1797-1874
Tune: William B. Bradbury, 1816-1868

88 88 Refrain
SOLID ROCK
www.hymnary.org/text/my_hope_is_built_on_nothing_less

# Reading 9: Psalms 32-34     Firm Forever

*The LORD foils the plans of the nations; but
the plans of the LORD stand firm forever.*     Psalm 33:10a; 11a NIV

As we look around us, it is easy to become disheartened and discouraged. Our world, in many ways, feels like it is spinning out of control, and it doesn't look to us like there is any easy way back.

That's when it is comforting to remind ourselves of the truth. Our God Almighty, maker of heaven and earth, is still – and forever will be – firmly in control. He is the One who simply spoke and the heavens came into being. He created all "their starry host by the breath of His mouth" (Psalm 33:6 NIV). Let's dwell on that one truth for a moment.

According to statistics from worldometer.com, the current world population is around 8 billion people. Scientific documents from physicsoftheuniverse.com report there are approximately 100 billion galaxies in just the observable universe, with an estimated minimum of 10 billion trillion stars. Some estimates are that there may be up to 200 billion trillion stars! But if we take just 10 billion trillion stars, and divide them among all 8 billion people on the planet, everyone would have over a trillion stars! And each was created simply by "the breath of His mouth". Imagine blowing your breath over your hand and 10 billion trillion stars are scattered throughout 100 billion galaxies! Absolutely incomprehensible, yet absolutely true.

The Gospel of John reveals this truth about Jesus: "In the beginning was the Word, and the Word was with God, and the Word was God. He was in the beginning with God. All things were made through Him, and without Him nothing was made that was made" (John 1:1-3). Also absolutely incomprehensible, yet absolutely true.

As we read today's Psalms to Him, let's rejoice that there is nothing and no one who is able to alter His plans and His purposes. Let's remind ourselves as we fervently pray that there is *absolutely nothing* too difficult for Him. The plans of Almighty God stand firm forever. Period.

# Leave It There

Charles Albert Tindley, 1916

Charles Albert Tindley

1. If the world from you with-hold of its sil-ver and its gold, And you
2. If your bo-dy suf-fers pain and your health you can't re-gain, And your
3. When your en-e-mies as-sail and your heart be-gins to fail, Don't for-
4. When your youth-ful days are gone und old age is steal-ing on, And your

have to get a-long with mea-ger fare, Just re-mem-ber, in His Word, how He
soul is al-most sink-ing in des-pair, Je-sus knows the pain you feel, He can
get that God in heav-en an-swers prayer; He will make a way for you and will
bo-dy bends be-neath the weight of care; He will ne-ver leave you then, He'll go

*Refrain*

feeds the lit-tle bird; Take your bur-den to the Lord and leave it there. Leave it there, leave it
save and He can heal; Take your bur-den to the Lord and leave it there.
lead you safe-ly through. Take your bur-den to the Lord and leave it there.
with you to the end. Take your bur-den to the Lord and leave it there.

there, Take your bur-den to the Lord and leave it there. If you trust and ne-ver doubt, He will

sure-ly bring you out. Take your bur-den to the Lord and leave it there.

# Reading 10: Psalms 35, 38       He Will Hear

*For in You, O LORD, I hope; You will hear, O LORD my God.*
Psalm 38:15

In today's two Psalms, David complains about the painful circumstances in his life, some due to the actions of others and some due to his own sin. In both Psalms, however, we find David leading us back from a focus on himself to a focus on our God.

In Psalm 35, David is extremely upset about other people wanting to harm him. He pleads with God to bring pain, destruction and judgment on his enemies. After 27 verses of complaining about his enemies, he changes his focus and says "My tongue will speak of Your righteousness and of Your praises all the day long" (Psalm 35:28).

Then in Psalm 38, David details the pain he is suffering as a result of his own actions, which he labels as "my sinful folly" (Psalm 38:5 NIV). Instead of pain from other people, he is experiencing the judgment of God because of his sin: "Your arrows pierce me deeply, and Your hand presses me down. There is no soundness in my flesh because of Your anger, nor any health in my bones because of my sin" (Psalm 38:2-3). But once again, David brings his focus back to the Lord. "For in You, O LORD, I hope; You will hear, O LORD my God" (Psalm 38:15).

As we turn our focus to Him again today in reading His Word and intercession, let's remember that in spite of any circumstance, we will find peace when we turn our focus back to our Almighty God. No matter what we face, whether a result of the actions of others, or our own foolishness and sin, the remedy cannot be found in ourselves. It can only be found in the Lord. Only He can right the wrongs; only He can bring forgiveness and healing; only He can restore the joy of our salvation. Because we know He hears and answers, let's take our burden to the Lord and leave it there.

# Under His Wings

1. Un - der His wings I am safe - ly a - bid - ing; Tho' the night
2. Un - der His wings, what a ref - uge in sor - row! How the heart
3. Un - der His wings, O, what pre - cious en - joy - ment! There will I

deep - ens and tem - pests are wild, Still I can trust Him; I
yearn - ing - ly turns to His rest! Of - ten when earth has no
Hide till life's tri - als are o'er, Shel - tered, pro - tect - ed, no

know He will keep me; He has re - deemed me, and I am His child.
balm for my heal - ing, There I find com - fort, and there I am blest.
e - vil can harm me; Rest - ing in Je - sus I'm safe ev - er - more.

*Chorus*

Un - der His wings, un - der His wings, Who from His love can sev - er?

Un - der His wings my soul shall a - bide, Safe - ly a - bide for - ev - er.

Words: W. O. Cushing
Music: Ira D. Sankey

PDHymns.com

# Reading 11: Psalms 36 & 37        Rest in the Waiting

*Rest in the LORD, and wait patiently for Him.* Psalm 37:7a

Sometimes we can read something without it really registering in our hearts and minds. "Rest in the Lord, and wait patiently for Him" can be one of those phrases. We can glance at it and say, "Yes, I agree." But what does it look like to rest in Him and wait patiently for Him?

There is much going on in the world around us that can cause us to be restless. Things are uncertain; people are unreliable; we feel vulnerable, unprotected. We don't know what the future holds and we don't like that feeling of not being in control. But the truth is that even when things felt certain, when we felt we could rely on people and we felt protected and secure, we weren't any more in control than we are right now. We just *felt* like we had control. People have had their lives turned upside down in the blink of an eye since time began.

David tells us that fretting or worrying about our circumstances only causes us harm (Psalm 37:8). Instead, he tells us to rest in the Lord and wait patiently for Him. What David is saying is to get our eyes off our circumstances (which are *always* beyond our control), and lift our focus to the Lord (who is *always* in control).

David goes on to tell us how to keep that perspective: he says to wait *patiently*. He knows better than to just tell us to wait. How impatient we can be in the waiting! And how disturbing that impatience is to our peace.

So, as we read these Psalms to the Lord today and fervently intercede, let's choose to rest in Him, our sovereign God. Let's determine to wait *patiently* for Him, casting *all* our care on Him, because He cares for us (I Peter 5:7). And let's choose to rest in the protection He offers to our hearts and minds as we take refuge under the shadow of His wings (Psalm 36:7).

# When We All Get to Heaven

1. Sing the won-drous love of Je - sus; sing his mer - cy
2. While we walk the pil - grim path - way, clouds will o - ver -
3. Let us then be true and faith - ful, trus - ting, ser - ving
4. On - ward to the prize be - fore us! Soon his beau - ty

and his grace. In the man - sions bright and bles - sed
spread the sky; but when trave - ling days are o - ver,
ev - ery day; just one glimpse of him in glo - ry
we'll be - hold; soon the pear - ly gates will o - pen;

*Refrain*

he'll pre - pare for us a place.
not a sha - dow, not a sigh.
will the toils of life re - pay.      When we all      get to
we shall tread the streets of gold.

hea - ven, what a day of re - joic - ing that will be!

When we all      see Je - sus, we'll sing and shout the vic - to - ry!

Text: Eliza E. Hewitt, 1898
Tune: Emily D. Wilson, 1898

87 87 Refrain
HEAVEN
www.hymnary.org/text/sing_the_wondrous_love_of_jesus_hewitt

# Reading 12: Psalms 39-41                    Just A Vapor

*Certainly every man at his best state is but vapor.* Psalm 39:5c

We don't like to think of our lives as just a vapor, but what exactly is a vapor? It is here one moment, and gone the next. And like a spray of cologne, it can be pleasingly powerful in the moment. It is not simply *nothing*; it's just not long-lasting. That may be a profitable perspective regarding our lives.

Our days are limited, passing quickly, here today and gone tomorrow. However, the Lord has purpose in the precise number of days He has allotted to each one of us. He instructs us to "redeem the time, because the days are evil" (Ephesians 5:16), so how do we do that?

First, we can be encouraged that Jesus' time of public ministry was only three years, so whatever time we have left can still be used to impact His kingdom. It's not the amount of time that is important. It's how we allow Him to direct our time.

Secondly, we can diligently study and implement His Word, seeking to hear His voice and follow His direction. In the midst of trials, there are people who need to hear His gospel of love and forgiveness. We may be an encouragement to others as they watch us endure and remain faithful. For others, we may be the only "Bible" they ever read as we walk in love and forgiveness made possible only through the Holy Spirit living in us. We can determine to use the remaining days of our lives to bring glory to Him.

As we deal with this temporary life and the ravages of sin in this world, let's remember this is not our home. We are just passing through. In a moment, in the twinkling of an eye, every pain will be gone, every sorrow forgot, and we will spend a joyous eternity with each other and with our Redeeming Lord. May that truth energize us today as we fervently intercede on behalf of our loved ones, our nation and our world.

# Praise Him! Praise Him!

Words by Fanny J. Crosby
Music by Chester G. Allen

# Reading 13: Psalms 42-45          Like a Yo-Yo

*Why are you cast down, O my soul? Hope in God...*     Psalm 42:5a, c

The theme of "Why are you down? Look up!" is repeated at least three times in our Psalm reading for today, so let's spend a little time with it.

We all know that it is a "downer" when we focus on our world and our circumstances. This life can never be paradise because of sin.

We also know that we should "look up", knowing that this life is as temporary as a vapor, that we are aliens in this world, and that we are just passing through on our way to our permanent home in heaven, where Jesus is preparing a place for us (John 14:2).

But if we know all of these truths, why do we often struggle with the constant "yo-yo" of having to turn our "downs" into "ups"?

If we could just make it a "one and done" proposition, never to struggle again, we would feel so good, so proud of ourselves, and think "I've got this." Instead, the continuing "down and up" is a helpful reminder that we always need the Lord, so let's embrace it.

Our Psalms today also remind us that help does not come from ourselves. We cannot save ourselves. It is only God's arm, God's strength, God's power (Psalm 44:3). Amazingly, however, He gives us the privilege of bringing about His kingdom through prayer. Our fervent intercession is exactly what we are supposed to do in order to bring His change in this world for His kingdom purposes. But it's all by God's power, not ours. Why? So He gets all the praise and all the glory.

The remedy repeated throughout our Psalms today is: "Hope in God, for I shall *yet* praise Him" (Psalm 42:5 – emphasis added). What a helpful and hopeful instruction to our souls. It speaks of a time that we can *know* is coming, a time of deliverance and rejoicing. It is future-focused, acknowledging that our all-powerful, all-wise God is working *all* things out in His way, in His time and for His glory.

# Rock of Ages

ISAIAH 26:4
Augustus M. Toplady, 1776

TOPLADY
Thomas Hastings, 1830

1. Rock of Ag - es, cleft for me, Let me hide my - self in Thee;
2. Not the la - bor of my hands Can ful - fill Thy law's de - mands;
3. Noth - ing in my hand I bring, Sim - ply to Thy cross I cling;
4. While I draw this fleet - ing breath, When my eyes shall close in death,

Let the wa - ter and the blood, From Thy wound - ed side which flowed,
Could my zeal no res - pite know, Could my tears for - ev - er flow,
Na - ked, come to Thee for dress; Help - less, look to Thee for grace;
When I rise to worlds un - known, And be - hold Thee on Thy throne,

Be of sin the dou - ble cure, Save from wrath and make me pure.
All for sin could not a - tone; Thou must save, and Thou a - lone.
Foul, I to the foun - tain fly; Wash me, Sav - ior, or I die.
Rock of Ag - es, cleft for me, Let me hide my - self in Thee.

# Reading 14: Psalms 46-49                    Even Then...

*Therefore we will not fear, though the earth give way...*Psalm 46:2 NIV

Today's Psalm reading begins with these powerful words: "God is our refuge and strength, an ever-present help in trouble. Therefore we will not fear, though the earth give way and the mountains fall into the heart of the sea, though its waters roar and foam and the mountains quake with their surging" (Psalm 46:1-3 NIV). That's a pretty dramatic turning upside down of our world.

After describing this chaotic scenario, God says He will help "just at the break of dawn" (Psalm 46:5). What is "the break of dawn"? It marks the end of night. When our lives feel like we are in the darkest of nights, take courage; He promises He is coming "just at the break of dawn."

Psalm 46 continues with words describing our world today: "Nations are in uproar, kingdoms fall;" but then comforts with these words: "Come behold the works of the LORD. He makes wars cease to the end of the earth; He breaks the bow and cuts the spear in two; He burns the chariot in the fire" (Psalm 46:6-9). Talk about our God taking an active role in the affairs of men!

Surprisingly, the very next verse is God's familiar directive to be still: "Be still, and *know* that I am God" (Psalm 46:10 – emphasis added). Sometimes it feels as though our world is crashing in around us. For some of us, it literally may be. Some of us may be suffering persecution or famine, with suffering and death on every side. But God says, *even then*, we can choose not to be afraid, because He is on His holy throne as He reigns and rules the nations (Psalm 47:8). Nothing and no one can thwart His plans, which include these momentary trials that are working for us "a far more exceeding and eternal weight of glory" (II Corinthians 4:17).

As we come before Him today, let's quiet our minds in the midst of our circumstances and speak truth to our hearts. Through all the storms of this temporary life, though it may feel at times like the earth beneath our feet is giving way, nothing takes Him by surprise, and He is with us *always*, in every moment, "even to the end of the age" (Matthew 28:20).

# Grace Greater Than Our Sin

Text: Julia H. Johnston, 1849-1919
Tune: Daniel B. Towner, 1850-1919

99 99 Refrain
MOODY
www.hymnary.org/text/marvelous_grace_of_our_loving_lord

# Reading 15: Psalms 50-52 Steadfast

*Create in me a clean heart, O God, and
renew a steadfast spirit within me.* Psalm 51:10

Psalm 51 was written after the prophet Nathan confronted David about his adultery with Bathsheba. Not only did David commit adultery, but then he committed murder to cover up his adultery. How could God forgive someone guilty of such grievous sins?

Decades before, God had rejected Saul as king. Why? Because Saul had not waited for Samuel before Saul made a sacrifice to the Lord. It seems like such a small thing to us, but it caused God to take away Saul's kingdom and give it to "a man after His own heart" – the humble shepherd David (I Samuel 13:14).

Did God not know that David would commit adultery, as well as a cover-up murder, during his reign as king? Of course, He did. So why did God reject Saul for such a little thing, but forgive David for such grave sins? That doesn't make sense to us. Why? Because we like to rank sins, judging some sins as worse than others.

Thankfully, God doesn't judge us by our sins. God says "man looks at the outward appearance" but He "looks at the heart" (I Samuel 16:7). The difference between Saul and David was the condition of their heart. After acknowledging his sin, David had "a broken and a contrite heart" (Psalm 51:17).

We can rejoice that, no matter how grievous, *no* sin is unforgiveable - if we come to Him in repentance. Then He lovingly says our sins are forgiven; so "go and sin no more" (John 8:11). Then He can restore to us a spirit that is determined to be steadfast in living a life pleasing to Him (Psalm 51:10).

May these truths encourage us as we read these Psalms and fervently intercede on behalf of all those blinded by the deceptions of the enemy. May the Lord break our hearts for the lost and give His light "to those who sit in darkness and the shadow of death" (Luke 1:79).

# Day by Day

2 CORINTHIANS 4:16
Karolina W. Sandell-Berg, 1865; *tr. by* Andrew L. Skoog

BLOTT EN DAG
Oskar Ahnfelt, 1872

1. Day by day, and with each pass-ing mo-ment, Strength I find, to meet my tri-als here;
2. Ev-ry day, the Lord Him-self is near me With a spe-cial mer-cy for each hour;
3. Help me then in ev-ry trib-u-la-tion, So to trust Thy prom-is-es, O Lord,

Trust-ing in my Fa-ther's wise be-stow-ment, I've no cause for wor-ry or for fear.
All my cares He fain would bear, and cheer me, He Whose Name is Coun-se-lor and Pow'r.
That I lose not faith's sweet con-so-la-tion, Of-fered me with-in Thy ho-ly Word.

He Whose heart is kind be-yond all meas-ure Gives un-to each day what He deems best—
The pro-tec-tion of His child and treas-ure Is a charge that on Him-self He laid;
Help me, Lord, when toil and trou-ble meet-ing, E'er to take as from a fa-ther's hand,

Lov-ing-ly, its part of pain and pleas-ure, Min-gling toil with peace and rest.
"As thy days, thy strength shall be in meas-ure," This the pledge to me He made.
One by one, the days, the mo-ments fleet-ing, Till I reach the prom-ised land.

# Reading 16: Psalms 53-56      Tears in a Bottle

*You number my wanderings; put my tears into Your bottle;*
*are they not in Your book?*      Psalm 56:8

A study of David's life reveals he had many times of great sorrow, including deep remorse for his sins of adultery and murder, painful wounds from the betrayal of friends, and intense grief with the death of two sons. He also had many times when he was fleeing for his life.

In the midst of these dark times, David reminds himself that God is not only powerful, but deeply personal. He sees; He keeps a record of our troubles and our tears.

When writing today's Psalms, David was hiding from King Saul (Psalm 54), was betrayed by friends (Psalm 55), and was a Philistine prisoner (Psalm 56). He had good reason to be fearful and downcast. He was not experiencing God's deliverance in, nor from, these moments. But he chooses to move his focus from his temporary trials to the trustworthiness of his God, and twice declares, "In God I have put my trust; I will not be afraid. What can man do to me?" (Psalm 56:4, 11)

If we are walking in fear today, let's follow David's example in Psalm 56:3: "Whenever I am afraid, I will trust in You." If we are carrying a burden today, David says "Cast your burden on the LORD and He shall sustain you" (Psalm 55:22). And with David, we can choose to rejoice, "For You have delivered my soul from death, yes, my feet from falling, that I may walk before God in the light of life" (Psalm 56:13 ESV).

Our God knows all the details of our lives, from beginning to end. Nothing is a surprise to Him. He not only knows the precise number of our days before we were born (Psalm 139:16), but He knows the exact number of every hair on our head (Luke 12:7). When we truly grasp how intimately He knows us and how deeply He loves us, we can more fully and completely trust Him with every detail of our lives.

# I Am Thine, O Lord

1. I am Thine, O Lord, I have heard Thy voice, And it told Thy
2. Con - se - crate me now to Thy ser - vice, Lord, By the pow'r of
3. O the pure de - light of a sin - gle hour That be - fore Thy
4. There are depths of love that I can - not know Till I cross the

love to me; But I long to rise in the arms of faith, And be
grace di - vine; Let my soul look up with a stead - fast hope, And my
throne I spend; When I kneel in prayer, and with Thee, my God, I com -
nar - row sea; There are heights of joy that I may not reach Till I

clo - ser drawn to Thee.
will be lost in thine. Draw me nea - rer, nea - rer, bles - sed
mune as friend with friend!
rest in peace with Thee.

Lord, To the cross where Thou hast died; Draw me nea - rer, nea - rer,

nea - rer, bles - sed Lord, To Thy pre - cious, bleed - ing side.

Text: Fanny J. Crosby, 1820-1915
Tune: William H. Doane, 1832-1915

10 7 10 7 Refrain
I AM THINE
www.hymnary.org/text/i_am_thine_o_lord_i_have_heard_thy_voice

# Reading 17: Psalms 57-59     It's All About Him

*Be exalted, O God, above the heavens;*
*let Your glory be above all the earth.*     Psalm 57:5

Psalms 57-59 were written by David when he was in extreme circumstances. He was in constant fear for his life because King Saul and his men were hunting him down to kill him. Can we even begin to imagine the fear, frustration and anger that David felt?

The young shepherd boy had become a hero in Israel because he had defeated the giant Goliath. But instead of being honored, he was hiding in caves, hunted down, running for his life. Why? All because of jealousy and envy. Saul could not stand David's popularity, so he ordered his death. At times, Saul even accompanied his men in search of David.

David had every reason to be frustrated with God's timing and to be angry with God. It appeared as if God was not doing anything to right the wrongs and rescue him. But that did not deter David's trust in the Lord. In the midst of his difficulties, David says "My soul trusts in You; and in the shadow of Your wings I will make my refuge, until these calamities have passed by" (Psalm 57:1).

David did not deny his circumstances. But David understood that God's purposes outweigh any temporary trials we face. After listing his troubles, he immediately shifts his focus to the eternal purposes of God: "Be exalted, O God, above the heavens; let Your glory be above all the earth." David is essentially saying "It's not about me; it's all about You."

This is the same mindset we find in Jesus prior to His crucifixion. After asking if the cup of suffering can pass, Jesus concludes with "Nevertheless, not My will, but Yours, be done" (Luke 22:42).

Let's ask the Lord today to help us move our focus from our temporary trials to His eternal purposes. What a privilege to be chosen, useful vessels for His kingdom and for His glory during our brief time here on earth. After all, it's all about Him.

# A Shelter In Time Of Storm

1. The Lord's our Rock, in Him we hide, A Shel-ter in the time of storm;
2. A shade by day, de-fense by night, A Shel-ter in the time of storm;
3. The rag-ing storms may round us beat, A Shel-ter in the time of storm;
4. O rock di-vine, O Ref-uge dear, A shel-ter in the time of storm;

Se-cure what-ev-er ill be-tide, A Shel-ter in the time of storm.
No fears a-larm, no foes af-fright, A Shel-ter in the time of storm.
We'll nev-er leave our safe re-treat, A Shel-ter in the time of storm.
Be thou our Help-er ev-er near, A shel-ter in the time of storm.

**Chorus**

O, Je-sus is a Rock in a wea-ry land, A wea-ry land, a wea-ry land;

O, Je-sus is a Rock in a wea-ry land, A Shel-ter in the time of storm.

Words by Vernon J. Charlesworth, Arr by Ira D. Sankey
Music by Ira D. Sankey

PDHymns.com

# Reading 18: Psalms 60-63                  Fill and Spill

*When my heart is overwhelmed,*
  *lead me to the rock that is higher than I.*          Psalm 61:2

When we hear the term "overwhelmed", we can easily identify with it, can't we? In this sin-ravaged world, our hearts can so easily become overwhelmed with anxiety, pain and disappointment.

It is during these times of fear, uncertainty and heartache that David encourages us to ask the Lord to lead us to the rock that is higher than our circumstances. That rock, that stability, that firm foundation is found in Him alone.

David further instructs us to "Trust in Him at all times, you people; pour out your heart before Him; God is a refuge for us" (Psalm 62:8). David doesn't say trust God some of the time; David says trust Him at *all* times. He encourages us to pour out our hearts to Him because He is our refuge, a place of safety and protection, our shelter in the time of storm.

What happens when we pour out our hearts to Him? We empty our hearts of our fears, our hurts, and our vain imaginings. An empty heart is a heart that He can then fill with His love, His peace and His comfort. Wouldn't we rather walk around with hearts filled with His love, peace and comfort instead of our own fear, worries and pain?

The beauty of having our hearts filled by Him is that these blessings can then spill over into the hearts of those He brings across our path. We can be used by Him to pour His comfort, His love, and His peace into the lives of others. *Fill and spill.*

As we run to Him and receive His protection, comfort and peace, we will discover with David that His overwhelming love is better than life itself (Psalm 63:3). Why? Because, in His audacious lovingkindness, He died to purchase our salvation, so that we will be able to live together with Him for all eternity (I Thessalonians 5:10).

# A Mighty Fortress

1. A might-y for - tress is our God, A bul-wark nev-er fail - ing;
2. Did we in our own strength con - fide Our striv-ing would be los - ing;
3. And tho' this world, with e - vil filled, Should threat-en to un - do us;
4. That word a - bove all earth - ly pow'rs, No thanks to them, a - bid - eth;

Our help - er He, a - mid the flood Of mor - tal ills pre - vail - ing.
Were not the right One on our side The Man of God's own choos - ing.
We will not fear, for God hath willed His truth to tri - umph thru us.
The Spir - it and the gifts are ours Thru Him who with us sid - eth:

For still our an - cient foe Doth seek to work us woe; His craft and pow'r are
Dost ask who that may be? Christ Je - sus, it is He; Lord Sa - ba - oth His
The prince of dark - ness grim, We trem - ble not for him; His rage we can en -
Let goods and kin - dred go, This mor - tal life al - so; The bod - y they may

great, And, armed with cru - el hate, On earth is not his e - qual.
name, From age to age the same, And He must win the bat - tle.
dure, For lo, his doom is sure, One lit - tle word shall fell him.
kill: God's truth a - bid - eth still, His king - dom is for - ev - er.

Words by M. L. Tr. By F. H. Hedge
Music by Martin Luther

PDHymns.com

# Reading 19: Psalms 64-66                    Our Mighty God

*By awesome deeds in righteousness You will answer us,*
*    O God of our salvation.*                    Psalm 65:5a

When we think of God, what do we imagine? Do we think of someone like a president or dictator, who orders people around and tells them what to do? Or do we think of an angry old man, wagging his finger at all the sinners in the world, just waiting to rain down fire and brimstone in judgment? Or maybe we imagine an inexplicable force of some type that miraculously set the universe in order, someone who just "wound up the clock" and then walked away.

None of those images fit the God of the Bible. In just our Psalms for today, David describes God as the One "who established the mountains by His strength, being clothed with power;" He stills "the noise of the seas, the noise of their waves, and the tumult of the peoples" (Psalm 65:6-7). David proceeds to declare, "How awesome are Your works! Through the greatness of Your power Your enemies shall submit themselves to You. All the earth shall worship You." David then invites us to "Come and see the works of God; He is awesome in His doing toward the sons of men. His eyes observe the nations; He rules by His power forever" (Psalm 66:3-7).

This is the God of the Bible. This is the powerful God we serve. This is the One who rebukes the winds and the waves. In gently chiding His disciples for their fear during the storm on the Sea of Galilee, Jesus asked "Why are you fearful, O you of little faith?" (Matthew 8:26). It was because they didn't really understand that He was God. They said "Who can this be, that even the winds and the sea obey Him?" (Matthew 8:27).

Let's remind ourselves today of how truly powerful our God is. As Creator, He simply spoke the entire universe into being. There is *nothing* too difficult for Him. In awesome deeds, He *will* answer us because He is the God of our salvation, our mighty God.

# God Will Take Care of You

1. Be not dis- mayed what- e'er be- tide, God will take care of you;
2. Through days of toil when heart doth fail, God will take care of you;
3. All you may need he will pro- vide, God will take care of you;
4. No mat- ter what may be the test, God will take care of you;

be- neath his wings of love a- bide, God will take care of you.
when dan- gers fierce your path as- sail, God will take care of you.
noth- ing you ask will be de- nied, God will take care of you.
lean, wea- ry one, up- on his breast, God will take care of you.

*Refrain*

God will take care of you, through ev- ery day, o'er all the way;

he will take care of you, God will take care of you.

Text: Civilla D. Martin, 1904
Tune: W. Stillman Martin, 1905

CM Refrain
MARTIN
www.hymnary.org/text/be_not_dismayed_whateer_betide

# Reading 20: Psalms 67 & 68        The Chariots of God

*The chariots of God are twenty thousand,*
*        even thousands of thousands;*                    Psalm 68:17

Our inclination is to think of God as just an observer of the affairs of men. We may feel it is all up to us to "straighten out this mess" in our world today. But David reminds us of the truth. Our God is in charge, and He can be trusted to provide for those looking to Him.

Our Almighty God "rides on the clouds, on the heaven of heavens"; He gives the word and "kings of armies flee"; He scatters "the peoples who delight in war". David puts the exclamation point on this topic by saying "The chariots of God are twenty thousand, even thousands of thousands" (Psalm 68:4, 11-12, 17, 30, 33).

The "chariots of God" image reminds us of Elisha and his fearful servant when surrounded by a massive Syrian army, as recounted for us in II Kings 6:16-17. Elisha tells his servant "Do not fear, for those who are with us are more than those who are with them." Then Elisha asks God to open the servant's eyes so he can see the army of God: "The mountain was full of horses and chariots of fire all around Elisha." God protected them far better than man ever could.

Accounts of God's miraculous protection are not limited to the Bible. One of the more recent examples is the testimony of Air Force Capt. Scott O'Grady, who was shot down over Bosnia in 1995. Enemy soldiers saw him parachute to the ground and walked right by him twenty minutes later. Even though it was broad daylight, they did not see him. He gives God all the glory for supernaturally protecting him.[14]

Let's remind ourselves again of the truth: our God remains firmly in control, even when it may not look that way to our earthly eyes. Nothing and no one can thwart His plans. Not even a sparrow falls without His knowledge (Matthew 10:29), so we need not fear. No matter what our circumstances may be, our Heavenly Father knows and will care for us.

# Jesus Paid It All

1. I___ hear the Sa-vior say, "Thy stength in-deed is small,
2. Lord,___ now in-deed I find Thy pow'r and Thine a-lone,
3. For___ noth-ing good have I Where-by Thy grace to claim;
4. And___ when, be-fore the throne, I stand in Him com-plete,

Child of weak-ness, watch and pray, Find in Me thine all in all."
Can change the le-per's spots And___ melt the heart of stone.
I'll wash my gar-ments white In the blood of Cal-v'ry's Lamb.
"Je-sus died my soul to save," My___ lips shall still re-peat.

*Refrain*

Je-sus paid it all, All to Him I owe;

Sin had left a crim-son stain, He washed it white as snow.

Text: Elvina M. Hall, 1820-1889
Tune: John T. Grape, 1835-1915

Irregular
ALL TO CHRIST
www.hymnary.org/text/i_hear_the_savior_say_thy_strength_indee

# Reading 21: Psalms 69 & 70    His Reputation

*Let not those who seek You be confounded because of me...*

Psalm 69:6b

David spends most of his writing in today's Psalms bemoaning his circumstances. He complains to God about the unfairness of life, and asks God to come to his aid and bring destruction and judgment on his enemies. He is totally focused on His circumstances and crying out to God for relief.

But suddenly, in the midst of his bewailing, he tells the Lord "Let not those who seek You be confounded because of me" (Psalm 69:6b). He moves from being consumed about his own situation to being concerned about how his behavior might be affecting God's reputation. He willingly admits that He is not perfect, writing "O God, You know my foolishness; and my sins are not hidden from You" (Psalms 69:5).

Are we as equally concerned as David about how our behavior affects God's reputation? When people watch us in action, would they say we are more loving, more honest, more generous, and more forgiving than the rest of the world? Are we less selfish, less prideful, less gossipy, and less self-righteous than our non-Christian friends?

The most common criticism the world has about Christians is that they see us as hypocrites. They say our walk doesn't match our talk. Let's take that criticism to the Lord and ask if there is anything that we think, say or do in each one of our own lives that does not reflect well on Him.

As redeemed children of God, we desire to represent Him well. We do not want to be a stumbling block for people seeking Christ. We all want people to come to a saving knowledge of the truth (I Timothy 2:4).

But we are not perfect, and none of us ever will be, this side of heaven. So let's come before our Refiner, and ask Him to reveal any dross that may be marring a clear reflection of Him. Then let's confess, repent and rejoice that "He is faithful and just to forgive us our sins and to cleanse us from all unrighteousness" (I John 1:9).

# O The Deep, Deep Love Of Jesus

## EBENEZER

1. { O the deep, deep love of Je - sus! vast, un - mea - sured, bound - less, free, }
   { Roll - ing as a might - y o - cean in its full - ness o - ver me. }
2. { O the deep, deep love of Je - sus! spread His praise from shore to shore! }
   { How He lov - eth, ev - er lov - eth, chang - eth nev - er, nev - er - more! }
3. { O the deep, deep love of Je - sus! love of ev - 'ry love the best: }
   { 'Tis an o - cean vast of bless - ing, 'tis a ha - ven sweet of rest. }

Un - der - neath me, all a - round me, is the cur - rent of Thy love;
How He watch - eth o'er His loved ones, died to call them all His own;
O the deep, deep love of Je - sus! 'tis a heav'n of heav'ns to me;

Lead - ing on - ward, lead - ing home - ward, to Thy glo - rious rest a - bove.
How for them He in - ter - ced - eth, watch - eth o'er them from the throne.
And it lifts me up to glo - ry, for it lifts me up to Thee

Words: S. Trevor Francis (c. 1890)
Music: Thomas J. Williams (c. 1890)

# Reading 22: Psalms 71 & 72                    Precious

*...and precious shall be their blood in His sight.*        Psalm 72:14b

W e know that our God is so intimately acquainted with all of our ways that He knows every hair on our head, He knows the number of our days, He even knows our thoughts and the words we are about to say before we even say them (Psalm 139:4). So it shouldn't surprise us that our blood - which could be interpreted to represent our life and/or our death - is "precious in His sight."

That is a nearly unfathomable thought, isn't it? The God who spoke all the universe into being and holds all things together by the power of His word (Hebrews 1:3), is so personal that all the moments of each one of our lives, even our very blood, is *precious* to Him.

Oh, that we could truly grasp how wide and how long and how high and how deep is the love of God for each one of us (Ephesians 3:18-19). What a difference that could make as we face each fear, each trial, and each loss in this fleeting experience of life. It would make it so much easier to run to Him with every fear or anxious thought, to simply trust Him through every trial, and to be comforted by Him in every sadness and loss.

Let us remind ourselves that our old life has been crucified with Christ, and the new life we now live is Christ living in us (Galatians 2:20). Therefore, our life, which is now actually His life living in and through us, would, of course, be precious to Him. What an astonishing truth!

As we read Psalms 71 and 72 to the Lord today and stand in the gap in intercession, let's re-commit to using our lives to bring glory to Him in all we do (I Corinthians 10:31). And no matter what circumstance we face, let us continue to place our hope and trust in Him alone, because He alone is our rock, our refuge and our fortress (Psalm 71:1-3).

# Just A Closer Walk With Thee

1. I am weak but Thou art strong; Je - sus, keep me from all wrong.
2. Thru this world of toil and snares, If I fal - ter, Lord, who cares?
3. When my fee - ble life is o'er, Time for me will be no more,

I'll be sat - is - fied as long As I walk, dear Lord, close to Thee.
Who with me my bur - den shares? None but Thee, dear Lord, none but Thee.
Guide me gen - tly, safe - ly o'er To Thy king - dom shore, to Thy shore.

*Chorus*

Just a clos - er walk with Thee, Grant it, Je - sus, is my plea.

Dai - ly walk - ing close to Thee, Let it be, dear Lord, let it be.

Words by American Folk Song
Music by American Folk Song, Arr. by Mosie Lister

# Reading 23: Psalms 73 & 74        Hand In Hand

*You hold me by my right hand.* Psalm 73:23b

Sometimes, as adults, we feel we should be responsible for all things. It feels appropriate to worry, to try to control everything. But Jesus says that we need to become like little children if we want to see the kingdom of heaven (Matthew 18:3). He didn't mean we should become childish, acting immaturely or irresponsibly. He meant we should become *childlike* in trusting our Heavenly Father.

Let's take a moment to think back on our days as a child. Can we remember a special time when we were just walking hand in hand with a parent or trusted adult? Let's pull up that moment, complete with all its emotion, and dwell on it for a bit.

We probably were skipping along, joyful and content to be wherever we were at that moment. We didn't have a care in the world. We weren't worried about tomorrow; we didn't carry any guilt about yesterday's mistakes. We felt we could trust that we would be protected and provided for, and that was all it took to be content.

That's exactly the image described in Psalm 73. The writer rejoices that the Lord is near him at *all* times, holding him by the hand. Therefore, he can confidently say of the Lord "You will guide me with Your counsel, and afterward receive me to glory" (Psalm 73:24).

What a marvelous visual of the truth. As we walk hand in hand with Him, He will lead us through each day until He take us to glory. We just need to remind ourselves to stay connected to Him, our Vine, and turn to Him in childlike trust, especially when we are afraid.

If we are fighting fear or anxiety today, let's just lift up our hand to Him and commit to hold on. As we intercede, let's welcome His presence, allowing His peace and His strength to fill our trembling souls. Let's choose to walk by faith and not by sight (II Corinthians 5:7) until He takes us to glory, where we will be with Him for all eternity.

# Praise to the Lord, the Almighty

1. Praise to the Lord, the Al - migh - ty, the King of cre - a - tion!
2. Praise to the Lord, who o'er all things so won - drou - sly reign - eth,
3. Praise to the Lord, who doth pros - per thy work and de - fend thee;
4. Praise to the Lord, O let all that is in me a - dore Him!

O my soul, praise Him, for He is thy health and sal - va - tion!
Shel - ters thee un - der His wings, yea, so gent - ly sus - tain - eth!
Sure - ly His good - ness, and mer - cy here dai - ly at - tend thee.
All that hath life and breath, come now with prai - ses be - fore Him.

All ye who hear, Now to His tem - ple draw near;
Hast thou not seen How thy de - sires e'er have been
Pon - der a - new What the Al - migh - ty can do,
Let the A - men Sound from His peo - ple a - gain,

Praise Him in glad a - do - ra - tion.
Gran - ted in what He or - dain - eth?
If with His love He be - friend thee.
Gla - dy for aye we a - dore Him.

Text: German Hymn, Joachim Neander, 1650-1680;
    tr. Catherine Winkworth, 1827-1878, alt.
Tune: *Stralsund Gesangbuch*, 1665;
    harm. W. Sterndale Bennett, 1816-1875

Irregular
LOBE DEN HERREN
www.hymnary.org/text/praise_to_the_lord_the_almighty_the_king

# Reading 24: Psalms 75-77          Incomprehensible

*Who is so great a God as our God?*
    *You are the God who does wonders...*          Psalm 77:13b, 14a

The sun rises every morning and sets every night, and we tend to think "Of course it does." But when was the last time we really tried to comprehend the incomprehensible wonders of creation?

Here are a few mind-boggling facts to ponder:

The sun is around 93 *million* miles away from earth.[15] Can we even begin to fathom that distance? If we drove that distance at 65 miles per hour, non-stop, it would take a whopping 163 *years* to drive there! Even if we flew at 550 miles per hour, it would take nearly 20 years to arrive. Incomprehensible.

In completing its rotation once every 24 hours, our earth spins at a speed of about 1,000 miles per hour! How is it that this planet can be spinning at that speed, and yet we can experience perfectly still air and can walk around without feeling a thing? That wouldn't be the same experience if we were shot out of a cannon and hurtling through space at 1,000 miles per hour! Incomprehensible.

But that's not all. While our earth is rotating 1,000 miles per hour, it is also orbiting the sun at around 67,000 miles per hour. At the same time, the earth, the sun, and our entire solar system is circling around the center of the Milky Way galaxy at about 450,000 miles per hour! Plus, it is estimated that there are over 100 *billion* galaxies or more![16] Absolutely incomprehensible!

Our God spoke all of this into being with just the power of His voice (Genesis 1). When we feel overwhelmed by anything in this brief, temporary life on earth, let's shift our focus to the power and majesty of the God who has called each one of us "out of darkness into His marvelous light" (I Peter 2:9).

As we intercede today, let's remind ourselves we can entrust every detail of our lives to the One who not only calls all the stars by name (Psalm 147:4), but who numbers every hair on our head (Luke 12:7). Incomprehensible indeed.

# Great Is Thy Faithfulness

1 Great is thy faith-ful-ness, O God my Fa-ther,
2 Sum-mer and win-ter and spring-time and har-vest,
3 Par-don for sin and a peace that en-dur-eth,

there is no shad-ow of turn-ing with thee.
sun, moon, and stars in their cours-es a-bove
thine own dear pres-ence to cheer and to guide,

Thou chang-est not, thy com-pas-sions, they fail not;
join with all na-ture in man-i-fold wit-ness
strength for to-day and bright hope for to-mor-row,

as thou hast been, thou for-ev-er wilt be.
to thy great faith-ful-ness, mer-cy, and love.
bless-ings all mine, with ten thou-sand be-side!

Text: Thomas O. Chisolm, 1866–1960
Music: William M. Runyan, 1870–1957

Text and music: public domain

FAITHFULNESS
11 10 11 10 WITH REFRAIN

*Hymnary.org*

# Reading 25: Psalm 78          Memorial Stones

*Then they remembered that God was their rock,*
*        and the Most High God their Redeemer.*     Psalm 78:35

When we first read this verse, we rejoice! They remembered! But, upon closer examination, we may become discouraged as we consider it in its context.

This verse begins with *"Then* they remembered..." So what happened in the verse before? Verse 34 says "When He *slew* them, *then* they sought Him" (Psalm 78:34 – emphasis added). How sad that it took calamity to get their attention. But are we any different?

God has miraculously rescued each one of us as believers from the slavery of sin. Yet, how often do we forget? How often do we not trust His higher ways? Why do we want to reject His direction and commandments, and go our own way, thinking we know better?

God knows that we tend to so easily forget who He is and what He has done. That is why He instructs a constant retelling of His works and His commands: "Teach them diligently to your children, and talk of them when you sit in your house, when you walk by the way, when you lie down, and when you rise up" (Deuteronomy 6:7) – in other words, *all* the time. What happens as we recount His wonders and His instructions? We also remind ourselves of His power, His ways and His truth.

When the Israelites crossed the Jordan River on dry ground, God initiated the idea of "memorial stones". He instructed that rocks be taken from the dry riverbed as a reminder of His miraculous provision so that "the peoples of the earth may know the hand of the LORD, that it is mighty, that you may fear the LORD your God forever" (Joshua 4:24).

How can we create "memorial stones"? We can share stories of His faithfulness, journal answered prayers, create a "Faith Journal" for our children, or reread the many Bible stories of God's miraculous provision.

As we spend time with the Lord today, let's remind ourselves how He has miraculously delivered us. Let's ask Him to show us ways we can create "memorial stones" to remind not only ourselves, but generations to come, of His great faithfulness.

# Rescue the Perishing

Frances Jane (Fanny) Crosby, 1869

William Howard Doane

1. Rescue the perishing, care for the dying,
2. Though they are slighting Him, still He is waiting,
3. Down in the human heart, crushed by the tempter,
4. Rescue the perishing, duty demands it;

Snatch them in pity from sin and the grave; Weep o'er the erring one,
Waiting the penitent child to receive; Plead with them earnestly,
Feelings lie buried that grace can restore; Touched by a loving heart,
Strength for thy labor the Lord will provide; Back to the narrow way

lift up the fallen, Tell them of Jesus, the mighty to save.
plead with them gently; He will forgive if they only believe.
wakened by kindness, Chords that were broken will vibrate once more.
patiently win them; Tell the poor wand'rer a Savior has died.

*Refrain*

Rescue the perishing, care for the dying, Jesus is merciful, Jesus will save.

# Reading 26: Psalms 79-81          Tender Mercies

*...preserve those who are appointed to die;*          Psalm 79:11c

In 2021, 3.5 million lives were lost worldwide to Covid-19.[17] In response to the threat of Covid, the world virtually shut down to preserve life. But was Covid-19 the leading cause of death in 2021?

Actually, no. Abortion was.[18] In 2021, there were 42.6 million abortions worldwide.[19] There were over 10 times as many deaths from abortion than Covid. Where was the mobilization to preserve *these* precious lives?

People familiar with abortion will tell us an even more revealing truth: there are really two victims in abortion. Life is not only taken from a mother's womb, but life is also taken from her heart. Few people talk about a mother's heartbreak following an abortion, but guilt can haunt her for the rest of her life.

Why aren't we doing more to stop this harm to so many women who feel they have no other choice except to take an innocent life? Is it because we don't really want to be bothered? We say "Oh, isn't that sad," but think "It's not my problem." Why is that? Is it because, deep down, we truly don't care about anyone else's life? Or have we been subtly influenced by the ways of the world?

As we pray today, Let's ask Him to show us His heart on this sensitive issue. Let's allow Him to burden our hearts for *both* mother and child involved in these challenging circumstances. Let's ask Him to show us how to use our time and resources to "preserve those who are appointed to die."

Let's remember that we all have been tricked by Satan's deceptions at various times in our lives. We all have sinned and fallen short (Romans 3:23). Together we plead, "Oh, do not remember former iniquities against us! Let Your tender mercies come speedily to meet us" (Psalm 79:8). Then, as Jesus did for the woman caught in adultery, may we not condemn, but give grace and lovingly say "Go and sin no more" (John 8:11).

# Revive Us Again

1. We praise Thee, O God! for the Son of Thy love,
2. We praise Thee, O God! for Thy Spi - rit of light,
3. All glo - ry and praise to the Lamb that was slain,
4. Re - vive us a - gain; fill each heart with Thy love;

For Je - sus who died, and is now gone a - bove.
Who hath shown us our Sa - vior, and scat - tered our night.
Who hath borne all our sins, and hath cleans'd ev' - ry stain.
May each soul be re - kin - dled with fire from a - bove.

Hal - le - lu - jah! Thine the glo - ry. Hal - le - lu - jah! A - men.

Hal - le - lu - jah! Thine the glo - ry, Re - vive us a - gain.

Text: William P. Mackay,1837-1885
Tune: John J. Husband, 1760-1825

11 11 Refrain
REVIVE US AGAIN
www.hymnary.org/text/we_praise_thee_o_god_for_the_son_of

# Reading 27: Psalms 82-85 Revival

*Will You not revive us again, that Your people may rejoice in You?*
Psalm 85:6

What a wonderful prayer for revival!

First, it reveals the proper motive in praying for revival – that we would rejoice in Him. Oftentimes, we tend to focus on ourselves instead of Him. We want things to go back to the way they were because our lives felt more predictable and more comfortable.

But that ease of life may have been exactly what got us into trouble in the first place. We may have readily acknowledged the existence of God; we may have even felt we were truly worshipping and honoring Him. But the truth is, we didn't feel like we really needed Him.

However, with the growing upheaval in our own individual lives as well as the lives of many around our planet, we are becoming increasingly aware of our desperate need for Him. And that is exactly what He wants to accomplish, not only in our lives, but in the lives of people around the world.

Secondly, this verse acknowledges that revival comes from God alone, reminding us that only prayer can bring the change we desire. He alone is able to draw wayward hearts back to Him. This truth can help us as we pray over the spiritual condition of our country, as well as the waywardness of those we love.

As we pray for revival, let's also include the Psalm writer's additional request: "But let them not turn back to folly" (Psalm 85:8d). What a waste of our fervent prayers if, in the end, people simply return to their selfish, foolish and ungodly ways. Peter talks of this pattern, warning that "the latter end is worse for them than the beginning. For it would have been better for them not to have known the way of righteousness, than having known it, to turn from the holy commandment delivered to them" (II Peter 2:20-21). May these truths encourage us to more fervently intercede for revival today.

# All To Jesus I Surrender

1. All to Je - sus, I sur - ren - der, All to Him I free - ly give;
2. All to Je - sus, I sur - ren - der, Humb - ly at His feet I bow;
3. All to Je - sus, I sur - ren - der, Make me, Sav - ior, whol - ly Thine;
4. All to Je - sus, I sur - ren - der, Lord, I give my - self to Thee;

I will ev - er love and trust Him, In His pres - ence dai - ly live.
World - ly pleas - ures all for - sak - en, Take me, Je - sus, take me now.
Let me know the joy of liv - ing, Tru - ly know that Thou art mine.
Fill me with Thy love and pow - er, Let Thy bless - ings fall on me.

**Chorus**

I sur - ren - der all, I sur - ren - der all;
I sur - ren - der all, I sur - ren - der all;

All to Thee, my bles - sed Sav - ior, I sur - ren - der all.

Words by J. W. Van De Venter
Music by W. S. Weeden

# Reading 28: Psalms 86-88          An Undivided Heart

*Give me an undivided heart, that I may fear Your name.*
Psalm 86:11 NIV

If we need to ask God for an *undivided* heart, we can assume that it does not come to us naturally. We likely more easily identify with a *divided* heart, torn between two opposing affections such as good and evil, or obedience and disobedience.

This is the same struggle Paul addressed when he said "For the good that I *will* to do, I do not do; but the evil I will *not* to do, that I practice. O wretched man that I am! Who will deliver me...? [Only] Jesus Christ, our Lord!" (Romans 7:19, 24-25 – emphasis added)

The truth is, we are born with a heart that is totally inclined to evil, that is "desperately wicked" (Jeremiah 17:9). Then God called us "out of darkness into His marvelous light" (I Peter 2:9), and He created a desire in our hearts to want to please Him. But we still struggle with wanting to only please ourselves. Our hearts are torn, divided.

In contrast, an undivided heart is one that is united in its direction of affection. It turns its focus first to God's kingdom and His righteousness, and leaves the rest to Him (Matthew 6:33). Whenever "the worries of this life and the deceitfulness of wealth" try to choke out our faith (Matthew 13:22 NIV), an undivided heart will fight to bring its focus back to His kingdom and His righteousness. A united heart also allows us to wholeheartedly seek His face in intercession on behalf of others, and will produce an abundance of fruit for the kingdom.

As we intercede today, let's ask Him for an undivided heart so that we can remain focused on the awesomeness and faithfulness of our Almighty God. No matter what uncertainty, fear and upheaval is going on in the temporary circumstances of our lives, our undivided heart can bring us back to a focus on this eternal truth – we have an all-powerful, all-knowing, all-sovereign God who is on our side (Romans 8:31).

# I Will Sing of the Mercies

WORDS: Psalm 89.1
MUSIC: James H. Fillmore, 1849-1936

I WILL SING
Irregular

*Hymnary.org*

# Reading 29: Psalm 89                                    The Gift

*I will sing of the mercies of the LORD forever...*Psalm 89:1a

$M$ercy is not a commonly used word today, so what exactly does it mean in this verse? It means not getting the punishment we justly deserve. What do we deserve? Death. Why? Because we all have sinned, and the penalty for sin is death (Romans 3:23; 6:23).

Today's Psalm says "Righteousness and justice are the very foundation of Your throne" (Psalm 89:14). Therefore, it is absolutely impossible for God to turn a blind eye to sin. We would like Him to, but that is not at all biblical. The righteousness and justice of God require the penalty of death for sin be paid, and paid *in full.*

We can only begin to appreciate the magnitude of God's mercy as we try to comprehend the immensity of His righteousness. God is total purity. He is completely righteous and always just. Therefore, He takes unrighteousness (sin) very seriously. How seriously?

God is so serious about sin that He sent *Himself,* (in the form of the Jesus, the Son,) to live a perfect, sinless life among us, and suffer the agony of the worst death imaginable, in order to satisfy His *own* wrath and judgment against sin. What a magnificent plan by which both His infinite mercy could be shown and his righteous justice be met in full.

Have we ever really taken the time to ponder this truth? Because of His great love for us, God *Himself* took on our sins and paid our penalty of death in order to redeem us and restore us to a right relationship to Him. How incomprehensible!

As we read Psalm 89 and engage in battle today, let's remember that there is no hope for anyone without Jesus. No one can earn their own salvation or work their way to heaven. We all have sinned, but Jesus paid it all. "The *gift* of God is eternal life through Christ Jesus our Lord" (Romans 6:23b KJV). If we confess to Him that we are sinners and receive His free gift of eternal life, we also will sing of the mercies of the Lord *forever!*

# Like a River Glorious

Words: Frances R. Havergal
Music: James Mountain

PDHymns.com

# Reading 30: Psalms 90-92                    Peace

*Whoever dwells in the shelter of the Most High*
*    will rest in the shadow of the Almighty.*   Psalm 91:1 NIV

Imagine for a moment a rushing waterfall. Take in the sights and sounds of the crashing, powerful water, coming wave upon wave. But then, on closer observation, you notice a little bird settled on her nest behind the waterfall. In spite of the turmoil and noise around her, she has found a place of security and protection, a place of peace and rest.

This image is similar to what the Psalmist describes in Psalm 91. No matter the circumstances swirling around us, we can choose to dwell "in the shelter of the Most High." And the result? We will experience "rest in the shadow of the Almighty." Rest in the shadow of the Almighty. Now that is truly a place of peace. What greater place of security and protection could there be than resting "in the shadow of the Almighty."

We tend to think of peace as the absence of trouble. But the peace that God gives is most profoundly experienced in the presence of turmoil. Jesus told us to expect trials and troubles in this world. That is the nature of our brief life on this earth. But what else did He say? He said that we can find our peace in Him, because He has overcome the world (John 16:33).

As we stand firm in our faith and engage the enemy in battle today, let us remind ourselves that "from everlasting to everlasting", He is God (Psalm 90:2b). Regardless of any circumstance we face, we can choose to dwell in the shelter of the Most High, and rest in the shadow of the Almighty.

And how can we remain in that place of peace? By continually giving thanks and singing praises to Him; "to proclaim Your love in the morning, and Your faithfulness at night" (Psalm 92:2). This turns our focus from the temporary troubles and turmoil of this world to our peace and rest promised in the shelter of the Most High.

# All The Way My Savior Leads Me

1. All the way my Sav-ior leads me; What have I to ask be-side?
2. All the way my Sav-ior leads me, Cheers each wind-ing path I tread,
3. All the way my Sav-ior leads me; O, the full-ness of His love!

Can I doubt His ten-der mer-cy, Who thru life has been my guide?
Gives me grace for ev-'ry tri-al, Feeds me with the liv-ing bread.
Per-fect rest to me is prom-ised In my Fa-ther's house a-bove.

Heav'n-ly peace, di-vin-est com-fort, Here by faith in Him to dwell!
Tho' my wea-ry steps may fal-ter, And my soul a-thirst may be,
When my spir-it, clothed im-mor-tal, Wings its flight to realms of day,

For I know, what-e'er be-fall me, Je-sus do-eth all things well; well.
Gush-ing from the Rock be-fore me, Lo! A spring of joy I see; see.
This my song thru end-less a-ges: Je-sus led me all the way; way.

Words by Fanny J. Crosby
Music by Robert Lowry

# Reading 31: Psalms 93-96                    Anxiety

*When anxiety was great within me,*
   *Your consolation brought joy to my soul.*   Psalm 94:19 NIV

When circumstances begin to fill us with fear, what consolations can calm our anxious minds and bring joy to our souls? The very first absolute bedrock of consoling truth is "Be still, and know that I am God" (Psalm 46:10). When anxiety begins to disturb our peace, this verse can immediately quiet our souls.

What else can cast out fear? Perfect love (I John 4:18). Who has perfect love for us? Our Lord and Savior, Jesus Christ. And "neither death nor life, nor angels nor rulers, nor things present nor things to come, nor powers, nor height nor depth, nor anything else in all creation, will be able to separate us from the love of God in Christ Jesus our Lord" (Romans 8:38-39 ESV). *Nothing* can separate us from His love. Period.

Then let's remind ourselves that He alone knows the beginning from the end and every moment in between. He declared "I am the Alpha and the Omega...who is and who was and who is to come, the *Almighty*" (Revelation 1:8 – emphasis added). What a statement of power! *Nothing* is too difficult for Him (Jeremiah 32:17), and *nothing* takes Him by surprise. And He is coming again!

In the meantime, He has promised to work all things out for our good because we love Him, and are called for His purposes (Romans 8:28). He called us; He *chose* us (John 15:16). This truth is such a comfort. Because He chose us, He will preserve us until everything He has planned for us has been fulfilled (Psalm 138:7-8 ESV). Period.

As we read our Psalms to Him and intercede today, let's praise Him for all the truths He has given us in His Word. And when anxiety tries to sneak in to destroy our peace and steal our joy, let's send it sprawling as we defeat it with our sword of truth, His Word. Rejoicing because He has overcome the world (John 16:33), let's cast all our cares on Him because He cares for us (I Peter 5:7).

# My Faith Has Found a Resting Place

1. My faith has found a re-sting place, Not in de-vice nor creed:
2. E-nough for me that Je-sus saves, This ends my fear and doubt;
3. My heart is lean-ing on the Word, The li-ving Word of God,
4. My great Phy-si-cian heals the sick, The lost He came to save;

I trust the E-ver-li-ving One, His wounds for me shall plead.
A sin-ful soul I come to Him, He'll ne-ver cast me out.
Sal-va-tion by my Sa-vior's name, Sal-va-tion thro' His blood.
For me His pre-cious blood He shed, For me His life He gave.

I need no o-ther ar-gu-ment, I need no o-ther plea,_____

It is e-nough that Je-sus died, And that He died for me.

Text: Lidie H. Edmunds
Tune: Norwegian Folk Melody;
     arr. William J. Kirkpatrick, 1838-1921

86 86 Refrain
LANDÅS
www.hymnary.org/text/my_faith_has_found_a_resting_place

# Reading 32: Psalms 97-101                    Faith

*Worship the LORD with gladness;*
*come before Him with joyful songs.*   Psalm 100:2 NIV

Today's Psalms recount the power of God: He reigns; He preserves; He delivers. He is victorious; He answers; He executes revenge. He is our Creator; we are His sheep, He is our Shepherd. In response, we are told to rejoice, sing praises, give thanks; shout joyfully, exalt and praise His holy name.

But sometimes, we just don't feel like praising Him. We look around and it seems as though He is not present. We turn to Him but don't see answers, not even on the distant horizon. We feel as if our prayers go into a great void with no one there who cares.

What we need is a major dose of truth.

So let's ponder this for a minute: Is there such a thing as air? Of course! But have we ever actually seen even a speck of air? No. But we see what air does. We smile as leaves shimmer in the breeze; we watch clouds float lazily across the sky; we are mesmerized as snowflakes dance in the frosty air.

It's no different with God. Though we haven't *yet* seen Him physically, the effects of Him are all around us. We can look back at how our sins brought us to our knees, and how He raised us up to new life in Him. We know He removed our cold, selfish heart of stone and gave us a heart of love for Him and compassion for others (Ezekiel 36:26). And it's not like we haven't had miraculous answers to our prayers. We just forget to remind ourselves about them.

So how do we move beyond doubt and despair? We take action. As we intercede today, we remind ourselves that we walk by faith and not by sight (II Corinthians 5:7). We determine, regardless of our feelings, to "be thankful to Him, and bless His name." Why? Because, this is truth: "The LORD *is* good and His love endures *forever*; His faithfulness continues through *all* generations" (Psalm 100:5 NIV).

# Savior, Like a Shepherd Lead Us

1. Sa - vior, like a shep-herd lead___ us,___ Much we need Thy ten - der care;
2. We are Thine, do Thou be - friend___ us,___ Be the guar-dian of our way;
3. Thou hast pro-mised to re - ceive___ us,___ Poor and sin - ful though we be;
4. Ear - ly let us seek Thy fa - vor,___ Ear - ly let us do Thy will;

In Thy plea - sant pas-tures feed___ us,___ For our use Thy folds pre - pare;
Keep Thy flock, from sin de - fend___ us,___ Seek us when we go as - tray;
Thou hast mer - cy to re - lieve___ us,___ Grace to cleanse, and pow'r to free;
Bles - sed Lord and on - ly Sa - vior,___ With Thy love our be - ings fill;

Bles-sed Je - sus, bles-sed Je - sus, Thou hast bought us, Thine we are;
Bles-sed Je - sus, bles-sed Je - sus, Hear, O hear us when we pray;
Bles-sed Je - sus, bles-sed Je - sus, Ear - ly let us turn to Thee;
Bles-sed Je - sus, bles-sed Je - sus, Thou hast love us, love us still;

Bles-sed Je - sus, bles-sed Je - sus, Thou hast bought us, Thine we are.
Bles-sed Je - sus, bles-sed Je - sus, Hear, O hear us when we pray.
Bles-sed Je - sus, bles-sed Je - sus, Ear - ly let us turn to Thee.
Bles-sed Je - sus, bles-sed Je - sus, Thou hast loved us, love us still.

Text: Dorothy A. Thrupp, 1779-1847;
*Hymns for the Young*, 1836
Tune: William B. Bradbury, 1816-1868

87 87D
BRADBURY
www.hymnary.org/text/savior_like_a_shepherd_lead_us

# Reading 33: Psalms 102 & 103         Dust

*As a father has compassion on his children, so the LORD has compassion on those who fear Him; for He knows how we are formed, He remembers that we are dust.*      Psalm 103:13-14 NIV

Some of us may be offended by being considered just "dust". But these verses can actually be comforting. Why? Because we don't have to pretend, or perform, or prove anything. He has chosen to love us just because we are His, and nothing can separate us from His love (Romans 8:38-39).

Sometimes, in trying to be a better follower, we can become self-focused. We begin evaluating our actions, measuring our performance through our own eyes, and then can struggle with pride in our accomplishments. It makes us realize, no matter how hard we try, we will never meet God's standard. In and of ourselves, our "goodness" will never "earn" us salvation.

Does that mean we should not even try to please Him? No, but it changes our motivation. We can strive to please Him like a child desires to please a parent. Of course, sometimes we think we know better about what is best, silly children that we are. But after getting bruised from bumping into reality, we can run back to Him.

What a wonderful picture of the relationship we have with Him, our all-knowing, all-wise, all-loving Father. As His child, if we recognize that we are no longer walking in obedience, we can come running back, tell Him we're sorry, and He takes us back immediately. Why? Because He remembers we are dust. And He has chosen to redeem us and love us just the same.

As we come to Him in prayer today, let's each come as His little child. Let's thank Him for accepting us, not because we are perfect, but simply because He has chosen us to be His. Then, out of gratitude for His love and mercy, we can aim to love and please Him with all our heart, with all our soul, with all our mind, and with all our strength (Mark 12:30). Because He loves us so.

# I Will Sing the Wondrous Story

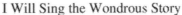

PSALM 89:1
Francis H. Rowley, 1886; *arr. by* Ira D. Sankey, 1887

Peter P. Bilhorn, 1886

1. I will sing the won-drous sto - ry Of the Christ Who died for me;
2. I was lost, but Je - sus found me, Found the sheep that went a - stray,
3. I was bruised, but Je - sus healed me, Faint was I from many a fall,
4. Days of dark - ness still come o'er me, Sor - row's path I of - ten tread,
5. He will keep me till the riv - er Rolls its wa - ters at my feet;

How He left His home in glo - ry For the cross of Cal - va - ry.
Threw His lov - ing arms a - round me, Drew me back in - to His way.
Sight was gone, and fears pos-sessed me, But He freed me from them all.
But His pres - ence still is with me; By His guid - ing hand I'm led.
Then He'll bear me safe - ly o - ver, Where the loved ones I shall meet.

*Refrain*

Yes, I'll sing the won-drous sto - ry, Of the Christ Who died for me,

Sing it with the saints in glo - ry, Gath-ered by the crys-tal sea.

*Hymnary.org*

# Reading 34: Psalms 104, 108                                Sing

*I will sing to the LORD as long as I live;*
*I will sing praise to my God while I have being.*   Psalm 104:33 ESV

There is something so very powerful about songs of praise. They allow our spirits to rise above our circumstances. They can bypass our emotions as our focus moves from ourselves to the truth of their words. They can lift a heavy heart out of a pit in almost miraculous and instantaneous ways.

The great reformer, Martin Luther, declared "Next to the Word of God, music deserves the highest praise. The gift of language combined with the gift of song was given to man that he should proclaim the Word of God through music."[20]

Song can reaffirm truth and minister to our souls unlike any other method. We can try looking at nature, and conclude that there has to be a God. We can read Scripture and agree that it is truth for our lives. But we sometimes can still struggle with translating that "head" knowledge into "heart" knowledge so it can impact the deepest part of our lives. Oftentimes, our hurt, confused, or troubled emotions can block that translation. But singing can minister truth directly, transforming our emotions, bringing comfort and healing to our deepest needs.

Pastor Charles Swindoll has said of the hymns: "For long centuries, its soothing strains have calmed anxious hearts, incited courage in the fainthearted, comforted the grieving, healed the wounded, rescued the perishing, and drawn wanderers home."[21]

No matter what may be troubling our souls today, let's choose to sing praise to Him in the midst of these trials. As we read the Psalms to Him, let's join the Psalmist in praising Him for His mighty deeds. As we choose to focus and keep our minds stayed on Him, He promises us perfect peace (Isaiah 26:3). Then let's take that peace which is independent of our circumstances (Philippians 4:7) into our intercession, confident that He is on His throne awaiting our requests so that His heavenly hosts can be released to accomplish His will, in His time and in His way.

# I Sing The Mighty Power Of God

1. I sing the might-y pow'r of God, That made the moun-tains rise;
2. I sing the good-ness of the Lord, That filled the earth with food;
3. There's not a plant or flow'r be-low, But makes Thy glo-ries known;

That spread the flow-ing seas a-broad, And built the loft-y skies.
He formed the crea-tures with His word, And then pro-nounced them good.
And clouds a-rise, and tem-pests blow, By or-der from Thy throne;

I sing the wis-dom that or-dained The sun to rule the day;
Lord, how Thy won-ders are dis-played, Wher-e'er I turn my eye:
While all that bor-rows life from Thee Is ev-er in Thy care,

The moon shines full at His com-mand, And all the stars o-bey.
If I sur-vey the ground I tread, Or gaze up-on the sky!
And ev-'ry-where that we can be, Thou, God art pres-ent there.

Words by Isaac Watts
Music by Gesangbuch der Herogl, Württemberg

# Reading 35: Psalm 105                    Remember

> *Seek the LORD and His strength;*
> *Remember His marvelous works...*          Psalm 105:4a, 5a

When facing difficult, painful or anxious circumstances, we tend to look to ourselves and our own strength. We can feel helpless and hopeless as our eyes focus only on our circumstances. Our minds can become filled with fear, doubt and despair. That's why the Psalmist instructs us to look to the LORD and *His* strength.

How can we most easily move our eyes from ourselves to the Lord and His strength? By filling our minds with all the *wonders* He has done.

He is the God of all creation, who simply spoke the entire universe into being. He is the God who, with mighty signs and wonders, led His people out of Egypt and into the promised land. He is the God who chose to come down to earth to live a perfect life among us and die an unspeakably agonizing, substitutionary death so that we could be credited with His righteousness and live forever with Him.

When we turn to Him in repentance and accept His free gift of salvation, He is the God who chooses to live in and through us. He is the God who reaches down into each of our lives, redeems us, and continues to draw us into intimate relationship with Himself. He is the God who promises to never leave us nor forsake us, who promises that nothing and no one can separate us from His love. This is the God we serve!

As we engage in battle today, let's remember that He alone is the God of wonder, power and might! Nothing is a surprise to Him and nothing is impossible for Him (Matthew 19:26). Let's release to Him any fear about where He is taking us or what our future holds. Let's also remember that, as we cry out to Him in fervent prayer, His answers may be the stories of miracles that will be told for generations to come, because He alone is the God of wonders.

# Take My Life and Let It Be

1 Take my life and let it be con-se-crat-ed,
2 Take my hands and let them move at the im-pulse
3 Take my voice and let me sing al-ways, on-ly,
4 Take my sil-ver and my gold; not a mite would

Lord, to thee. Take my mo-ments and my days; let them
of thy love. Take my feet and let them be swift and
for my King. Take my lips and let them be filled with
I with-hold. Take my in-tel-lect and use ev-ery

flow in end-less praise, let them flow in end-less praise.
beau-ti-ful for thee, swift and beau-ti-ful for thee.
mes-sag-es from thee, filled with mes-sag-es from thee.
power as thou shalt choose, ev-ery power as thou shalt choose.

5 Take my will and make it thine;
it shall be no longer mine.
Take my heart—it is thine own;
it shall be thy royal throne,
it shall be thy royal throne.

6 Take my love; my Lord, I pour
at thy feet its treasure store.
Take myself, and I will be
ever, only, all for thee,
ever, only, all for thee.

Text: Frances R. Havergal, 1874
Tune: H. A. Cesar Malan, 1827

77 77 with repeat
HENDON
www.hymnary.org/text/take_my_life_and_let_it_be

# Reading 36: Psalm 106        Mission Possible

*He saved them for His name's sake,*
*that He might make His mighty power known.*     Psalm 106:8

Have we ever stopped to think about what God's purpose was in saving us? We tend to think it's all about us: "He saved me from the penalty of my sin;" "He saved me so I could go to heaven;" "He saved me so I could have a better life here on earth." But according to Psalm 106:8, His purpose was to "make His mighty power known."

How can we make His mighty power known? First, we can share our testimony about how He saved us. I Peter 2:9 tells us to "proclaim the praises of Him who called you out of darkness into His marvelous light." But then it instructs "Live such good lives among the pagans...that they may see your good works and glorify God" (I Peter 2:12 NIV). We are to live such exemplary lives that nonbelievers will give glory to God for our good works and godly life. Now, that's a tall order!

Remember Mission Impossible? As Christians, our mission - which we have chosen to accept - is not about us. It's solely about bringing *Him* glory. But how can we remember to do this in our daily lives?

Let's try this: think "Pleasing Him" as we consider our myriad of choices each day. We can even add a question mark: "Pleasing Him?" as we evaluate each decision about our language, our dress, our attitude, our business practices, our relationships, our priorities for time or resources. This phrase helps bring our focus back to Him and our mission in life.

Let's ask the Lord to help us remember why He saved us. As we apply "Pleasing Him" to each decision, prepare to be amazed at how quickly this phrase can help our "walk" match our "talk". But let's also be prepared to experience what peace and joy it brings to our days as we constantly and consistently remind ourselves to stay on mission: "to make His mighty power known."

# Redeemed, How I Love to Proclaim It

Text: Fanny J. Crosby, 1820-1915
Tune: William J. Kirkpatrick, 1838-1921

98 98 Refrain
REDEEMED
www.hymnary.org/text/redeemed_how_i_love_to_proclaim_it

# Reading 37: Psalms 107, 110                    Redeemed

*Who is wise? Let him observe and heed these things;*
*and thoughtfully consider the lovingkindness of the LORD.*
Psalm 107:43 AMP

W e often say "People just need to come to the end of themselves."
We might even think this is a new concept. But this idea goes all the way
back to the time of Psalms. Psalm 107:4-28 (NIV) detail many examples
of fools who rejected God's ways but then came to the end of themselves.

Some "wandered in desert wastelands," hungry and thirsty. *Then,*
they cried out to the Lord and He delivered them. Others "sat in
darkness, in utter darkness" and the deepest depression because they
"rebelled against God's commands" and despised His plans. *Then,* they
cried out to the Lord and He saved them.

Some "became fools through their rebellious ways and suffered
affliction because of their iniquities; ...they drew near the gates of death."
*Then,* they cried out to the Lord and He healed them and "rescued them
from the grave." Others were caught up in storms and "were at their wits'
end." *Then,* they cried out to the Lord and He rescued them.

Doesn't this sound like lost people today? But the Lord gathers these
– His redeemed – "from the east and the west, from the north and the
south" (Psalm 107:3). This "great multitude which no one could number,
from all nations, tribes, peoples and tongues," will stand before the
throne and before the Lamb and cry out "Salvation belongs to our God
who sits on the throne, and to the Lamb!" (Revelation 7:9-10).

We are told that this countless multitude are those "who have come
out of the great tribulation." "Never again will they hunger; never again
will they thirst." and "God will wipe away every tear from their eyes"
(Revelation 7: 14, 16, 17 NIV).

What an encouragement as we go into intercession today. There are
countless people in our nation and from every nation, tribe and tongue
that have yet to come to the end of themselves, cry out to God, and be
redeemed. They are why we have answered this call to battle. May we
fight on with renewed intensity!

# Wonderful Words Of Life

1. Sing them o - ver a - gain to me, Won - der - ful words of Life;
2. Christ, the bless - ed One, gives to all, Won - der - ful words of Life;
3. Sweet - ly ech - o the gos - pel call, Won - der - ful words of Life;

Let me more of their beau - ty see, Won - der - ful words of Life.
Sin - ner, list to the lov - ing call, Won - der - ful words of Life.
Of - fer par - don and peace to all, Won - der - ful words of Life.

Words of life and beau - ty, Teach me faith and du - ty;
All so free - ly giv - en, Woo - ing us to heav - en;
Je - sus, on - ly Sav - ior, Sanc - ti - fy for - ev - er;

**Chorus**

Beau - ti - ful words, won - der - ful words, Won - der - ful words of Life;

Beau - ti - ful words, won - der - ful words, Won - der - ful words of Life.

Words and Music: Phillip P. Bliss

*Glorious and majestic are His deeds; He has*
  *caused His wonders to be remembered;*  Psalm 111:3a, 4a NIV

Mention "David and Goliath", and most everyone knows the story. From Genesis through Revelation, we find recounted many "glorious and majestic deeds" of our God Almighty. Through the Bible, God has caused His wonders to be remembered for thousands of generations.

Some people say the Bible is so old, it must have been corrupted with time. But the Dead Sea Scrolls, discovered in 1947, demonstrate that, because of reverence for God's commands, our current Old Testament is incredibly accurate. The first century Jewish historian Josephus explained, "For, although such long ages have now passed, no one has ventured either to add, or to remove, or to alter a syllable; and it is an instinct with every Jew from the day of his birth to regard them as the decrees of God."[22]

Similarly, the accuracy of our New Testament is upheld by the volume of ancient manuscripts that, with remarkable consistency, recount the Apostles' eye-witness accounts and teachings. James MacDonald documents, "There are now more than 5,600 ancient manuscripts of the Greek New Testament. Add to that nearly 10,000 Latin manuscripts and 9,300 other early versions, and we have nearly 25,000 early manuscripts of the Bible. No other ancient document even comes close. The next most commonly copied document is Homer's *Iliad,* with 643 manuscripts, all of them partial. Thus, the Bible manuscripts outnumber those for Homer by nearly forty to one."[23]

Although the Bible is the most authenticated, copied and most-read book of all time, people will still question its authenticity and authority. But we have every reason to trust it as the divinely inspired Word of God, remarkably preserved so that His wonders are remembered. As we read our Psalms to Him today, may we treasure His gift that has been faithfully passed down through the ages. May His "glorious and majestic deeds" bolster our courage as we intercede today. What a mighty God we serve!

# Joyful, Joyful We Adore Thee

1. Joy - ful, joy - ful, we a - dore Thee, God of glo - ry, Lord of love;
2. All Thy works with joy sur - round Thee, Earth and heav'n re - flect Thy rays,
3. Thou art giv - ing and for - giv - ing, Ev - er bless - ing, ev - er blest,
4. Mor - tals join the hap - py cho - rus, Which the morn - ing stars be - gan;

Hearts un - fold like flow'rs be - fore Thee, Open - ing to the sun a - bove,
Stars and an - gels sing a - round Thee, Cen - ter of un - bro - ken praise;
Well - spring of the joy of liv - ing, O - cean - depth of hap - py rest!
Fa - ther love is reign - ing o'er us, Broth - er love binds man to man.

Melt the clouds of sin and sad - ness; Drive the dark of doubt a - way;
Field and for - est, vale and moun - tain, Flow - ery mead - ow, flash - ing sea,
Thou our Fa - ther, Christ our broth - er, All who live in love are Thine;
Ev - er sing - ing, march we on - ward, Vic - tors in the midst of strife,

Giv - er of im - mor - tal glad - ness, Fill us with the light of day!
Chant - ing bird and flow - ing foun - tain Call us to re - joice in Thee.
Teach us how to love each oth - er, Lift us to the joy di - vine.
Joy - ful mu - sic leads us sun - ward In the tri - umph song of life.

Words by Henry van Dyke
Music by Ludwig van Beethoven, Arr. by Edward Hodges

# Reading 39: Psalms 113-115        Hallel (Part 1)

*Who is like the LORD our God,*
*     the One who sits enthroned on high...* Psalm 113:5 NIV

Our Psalms for today and tomorrow are known as "The Hallel". "Hallel" simply means "praise" and is similar to the English word, hallelujah, meaning "Praise Yah" or "Praise Yahweh".

In the first three Hallel Psalms we will read for today, the recurring theme is praising the name of the Lord. Specifically, we are led in praising Him for who He is, for what He has done, and for what He will do.

First, He is "exalted over all the nations, His glory above the heavens" (Psalm 113:4 NIV). There is no one like our God. Therefore, we are not foolish to worship Him, because He is God Almighty, the creator and ruler of the entire universe!

Secondly, He has done great things in our lives. Psalm 114 talks about bringing His people out of bondage in Egypt. Similarly, each one of us can look to our own lives and praise Him for how He has brought us out of our own bondage to sin and rebellion. Additionally, He gave us a heart that desires to please Him above all else. Indeed, He has done great things!

Thirdly, Psalm 115 talks about what He will do. "You who fear the LORD, trust in the LORD; He is their help and their shield" (Psalm 115:11). This describes His rescuing us and defending us – both offense and defense. What more could we ask for! He is *everything* we need in every circumstance of life.

As we come before Him today, let's follow the pattern outlined in these Hallel Psalms for praising Him. He is always and forever enthroned on high, so we praise Him for who He is. He has done great things in our lives and the lives of others, so we praise Him for what He has done. He has promised to be our help and our shield, so we can praise Him for what He will do. "It is we who extol the LORD, both now and forevermore. Praise the LORD" (Psalm 115:18 NIV). It is all about Him.

# The Love of God

Frederick Martin Lehman, 1917

Claudia Lehman Mays

1. The love of God is great-er far, Than tongue or pen can ev-er tell; It goes be-yond the high-est star, And reach-es to the low-est hell; The guilt-y pair, bowed down with care, God gave His Son to win; His err-ing child He re-con-ciled, And par-doned from his sin.

2. When years of time shall pass a-way, And earth-ly thrones and king-doms fall, When men, who here re-fuse to pray, On rocks and hills and mount-ains call, God's love so sure, shall still en-dure, All mea-sure-less and strong; Re-deem-ing grace to A-dam's race— The saints' and an-gels' song.

3. Could we with ink the o-cean fill, And were the skies of parch-ment made, Were ev-ery stalk on earth a quill, And eve-ry man a scribe by trade, To write the love of God a-bove, Would drain the o-cean dry. Nor could the scroll con-tain the whole, Though stretched from sky to sky.

**Refrain**

O love of God, how rich and pure! How mea-sure-less and strong! It shall for-ev-er-more en-dure The saints' and an-gels' song.

# Reading 40: Psalms 116-118          Hallel (Part 2)

*Oh, give thanks to the LORD, for He is good!*
        *For His mercy endures forever.*        Psalm 118: 1

Today's reading is the second half of the six Psalms known as "The Hallel". The word "Hallel" is short for the Hebrew phrase "Hallelu Yah", which translates as "Praise the LORD".

The Hallel Psalms played a significant role in many of the Jewish holidays, but particularly in the Passover celebration. A portion of them would typically be sung prior to the Passover meal, and the remaining would be sung after the meal.

Most scholars believe that today's Psalms were sung by Jesus and His disciples after the Last Supper, a Passover meal, before they walked to the Mount of Olives and the Garden of Gethsemane, where Jesus would be betrayed and then arrested before being crucified (Matthew 26:30).

As we read Psalms 116-118 to the Lord today, let us remember that Jesus sang these very same Psalms as a hymn of praise. Unlike the disciples, He was fully aware of the pain and suffering He was about to endure. For us. So that, with His crucifixion, the debt of our sin would be been paid *in full* (Isaiah 53:5). And with His victory over death in His resurrection, we could be empowered to "walk in newness of life" (Romans 6:4).

As we approach the Throne of Grace today, may we move our eyes from our temporary troubles to Him, giving thanks and reminding ourselves that He is good. Regardless of our immediate circumstances which will not last, we can know that "His mercy endures forever." We may not begin to grasp why He allows the trials we are facing, but we can know that "His mercy endures forever." With Job, we can say "Though He slay me, yet will I trust in Him" (Job 13:15). And this we can know for certain: "You have delivered my soul from death" (Psalm 116:8), so we can join the countless multitudes in the heavenly chorus singing, "His mercy endures forever."

# Open My Eyes, That I May See

1. O-pen my eyes, that I may see   Glimp-ses of truth Thou hast for me;
2. O-pen my ears, that I may hear   Voi-ces of truth Thou send-est clear;
3. O-pen my mouth, and let me bear   Glad-ly the warm truth ev'-ry-where;

Place in my hands the won-der-ful key   That shall un-clasp and
And while the wave-notes fall on my ear,   Ev'-ry-thing false will
O-pen my heart, and let me pre-pare   Love with Thy chil-dren,

set me free;   Si-lent-ly now I wait for Thee,   Re-ady, my God, Thy
dis-ap-pear;   Si-lent-ly now I wait for Thee,   Re-ady, my God, Thy
thus to share;   Si-lent-ly now I wait for Thee,   Re-ady, my God, Thy

will to see;   O-pen my eyes, il-lu-mine me,   Spi-rit di-vine!
will to see;   O-pen my eyes, il-lu-mine me,   Spi-rit di-vine!
will to see;   O-pen my eyes, il-lu-mine me,   Spi-rit di-vine!

Text: Clara H. Scott, 1841-1897
Tune: Clara H. Scott, 1841-1897

Irregular
SCOTT
www.hymnary.org/text/open_my_eyes_that_i_may_see

# Reading 41: Psalm 119:1-56          Owner's Manual

*Open my eyes, that I may see wonderful things from Your law.*

Psalm 119:18

Psalm 119 was written to celebrate God's law. But when we first encounter the word "law", our initial reaction is usually not one of celebration. Why? Because we immediately think someone is trying to tell us what we *can't* do. That's why we need the Lord to open our eyes, so we can view His law as a wonderful thing, something to help us live our best life possible.

Let's think back to when we bought our first car. We pored over the owner's manual to learn how the car was designed and how to best utilize the newest and latest features. How arrogant it would be to disregard the owner's manual and think "Well, I don't need any instruction. I can figure it out myself."

It's the same way with us. God designed us and knows far better how we function best. That's why He inspired, and preserved, His owner's manual – the Bible - so we could live our most productive and fulfilled life.

As we think back to the times when we chose to do it our way, doing what felt right to us, we ended up going down a destructive path. Why? Because He is God and we are not. His mind is infinite and ours is not. His ways are higher than our ways. We need to study and commit to His ways, not ours. The question is not "Does His way make sense to me?" The question is only "Is this His way?"

As we read today's portion of Psalm 119 to Him, may we embrace its truth with our whole heart. Then, let's commit to follow His guidance in obedience, walking by faith and not by sight, and turn that strengthened faith into fervent intercession. As we line up our lives with His instructions in His owner's manual, we will experience the blessings of doing things His way, because His Word gives us life (Psalm 119:50).

# It Is Well with My Soul

1. When peace like a ri - ver, at - tend - eth my way, When sor -
2. Tho' Sa - tan should buf - fet, tho' tri - als should come, Let this
3. My sin, oh, the bliss of this glo - ri - ous tho't: My sin
4. And, Lord, haste the day when the faith shall be sight, The clouds

rows like sea bil - lows roll; What - e - ver my lot, Thou hast
blest as - su - rance con - trol, That Christ has re - gar - ded my
not in part, but the whole Is nailed to the cross and I
be rolled back as a scroll, The trump shall re - sound and the

taught me to say, It is well, it is well with my soul.
help - less es - tate, And hath shed His own blood for my soul.
bear it no more, Praise the Lord, praise the Lord, O my soul!
Lord shall des - cend, "E - ven so," it is well with my soul.

It is well _____ with my soul, _____ It is well, it is well with my soul.

It is well with my soul,

Text: Horatio G. Spafford, 1828-1888
Tune: Philip P. Bliss, 1838-1876

Irregular
VILLE DU HAVRE
www.hymnary.org/text/when_peace_like_a_river_attendeth_my_way

# Reading 42: Psalm 119:57-112                    Affliction

*It is good for me that I have been afflicted,*
*that I might learn Your statutes.*          Psalm 119:71

We all want our lives to be trouble-free. Why? We think we deserve it. After all, we are doing our best to follow Him and do His will, so why should we have to suffer the heartbreak of wayward spouses or children, the pain of persecution, or the sorrow of the loss of health or life?

The truth is that trials are not something we can prevent, even though, consciously or subconsciously, we often rehearse all the details in our minds and wonder what we could have done differently. We are missing the point.

In our focus verse today, affliction is praised for teaching us to look to His ways, depending on Him instead of ourselves. Hebrews 12:11 (NIV) further reinforces this idea: "No discipline seems pleasant at the time, but painful. Later on, however, it produces a harvest of righteousness and peace for those who have been trained by it."

Scott Hubbard of desiringgod.org writes: "I would like to think I could have made it safely to heaven on a smooth path, running straight and wide beneath bright skies. I would like to imagine I would remain faithful to God without the training rod of trouble. But in a world like ours, and with hearts like ours, some of God's best gifts come wrapped in the black box of trouble. They burden us, sometimes almost unbearably. But they also bend us toward the One whose steadfast love is better than life (Psalm 63:3)."[24]

Whatever troubles we are facing, our sovereign God has allowed them for His divine purposes. Let's ask Him to help us be soft clay in His Potter's hands, as He forms us into useful vessels to carry and reflect His glory. May we see that these trials are causing us to "become mature and complete", so that we will be able to "count it all joy" (James 1:2). In the end, He is our portion (Psalm 119:57). He is all we need.

# He Leadeth Me

1. He lead-eth me: O bless-ed tho't! O words with heav-'nly com-fort fraught!
2. Some-times 'mid scenes of deep-est gloom, Some-times where E-den's bow-ers bloom,
3. Lord, I would clasp Thy hand in mine, Nor ev-er mur-mur nor re-pine,
4. And when my task on earth is done, When by Thy grace the vic-t'ry's won,

What- e'er I do, wher-e'er I be, Still 'tis God's hand that lead-eth me.
By wa- ters still, o'er trou-bled sea Still 'tis His hand that lead-eth me.
Con- tent, what-ev-er lot I see, Since 'tis my God that lead-eth me.
E'en death's cold wave I will not flee, Since God thru Jor - dan lead-eth me.

*Chorus*

He lead-eth me, He lead-eth me, By His own hand He lead-eth me;

His faith-ful fol-low'r I would be, For by His hand He lead-eth me.

Words by Joseph H. Gilmore
Music by William B. Bradbury

PDHymns.com

# Reading 43: Psalm 119:113-176      Embrace the Reins

*Direct my steps by Your Word,*
*    and let no iniquity have dominion over me.*      Psalm 119:133

Imagine a horse and buggy. The driver wants to get home with the least amount of time and energy. He knows the best way to accomplish that.

The horse has no idea what the goal is or how to get there. He just wants to go his own way and look for water, grass, and a shady place to lay down. Without the reins and direction of the driver, the horse may never get home to the safety of the stall, to food and water, and to the pleasure of pasture in the cool of the evening.

Both we and the horse often resist the idea of reins. We think that, without reins, we will be able to get to the same destination in the same amount of time, but by taking our own path and experiencing the pleasure of our own willfulness along the way.

If we are honest, our willful ways always get us into trouble. Have they ever truly led to peace and fulfillment? Or did they lead us into heartache and heartbreak, addictions and pain?

As we look around, our hearts break as we see the chaos and despair that result from throwing off His reins in willful rebellion. Sadly, while we as Christians know better, there are many who don't even know "the way, the truth and the life" (John 14:6). They have never experienced the benefits of being under His authority and His direction.

As we spend our last day in Psalm 119, may our hearts be filled with gratitude to God for His law, our reins. And may we entreat Him to restore across our country an appreciation for His reins. He designed us. He alone can lead us in the way we should go. May our lives be examples to others of the blessing of embracing His reins. May we clearly demonstrate that He alone can be trusted, in the midst of the uncertainty and struggles of this life, to efficiently and effectively lead us home.

# Near To The Heart Of God

1. There is a place of qui - et rest, Near to the heart of
2. There is a place of com - fort sweet, Near to the heart of
3. There is a place of full re - lease, Near to the heart of

God, A place where sin can - not mo - lest, Near to the heart of God.
God, A place where we our Sav - ior meet, Near to the heart of God.
God, A place where all is joy and peace, Near to the heart of God.

**Chorus**

O Je - sus, blest Re - deem - er, Sent from the heart of

God, Hold us, who wait be - fore Thee, Near to the heart of God.

Words and Music by C. B. McAfee

# Reading 44: Psalms 120-126 Crosses

*Those who sow in tears shall reap in joy.* Psalm 126:5

We probably all can recite the words of Jesus: "If anyone desires to come after Me, let him deny himself, and take up his cross daily, and follow Me" (Luke 9:23). We hear that and think, "Yep, we need to take up our cross and follow You, Lord." And He promises that "My yoke is easy and My burden is light" (Matthew 11:30), right?

Then why doesn't it feel light? Is it because we are carrying the burden of other people's crosses? What about that spouse who has stopped going to church? Or that son or daughter who has become a prodigal? Or that grandchild who shows no interest in spiritual things? Are we carrying their crosses, too?

Yes, we should care about their spiritual waywardness. Yes, we should take it as a burden to the Lord, but then we need to leave it there. Easier said than done, right? Yes, but we can ask the Holy Spirit to show us when we are starting to take it back, worrying about their eternal destiny, or thinking we need to find a way to fix them.

We need to continually remind ourselves that no amount of worry, argument, logic, pressure, manipulation, or emotional appeal is going to change them. Why? Because it is a matter of the heart. And only God can change a heart.

As we read our Psalms to the Lord today, let's praise Him for the promise that those who sow in tears will reap in joy. As we intercede on behalf of those we love who are wandering off in sin, let us remember that the most loving and effective thing we can do for them is to bring them to The Cross. In doing fervent battle on their behalf, we may be sowing in tears, but His promise is a joyful end. As we bring them to the only One who can transform their hearts, may we experience that quiet rest that Jesus promised: "Come to Me, all you who are weary and burdened, and I will give you rest" (Matthew 11:28 NIV).

# And Can it Be That I Should Gain?

Text: Charles Wesley (1707-1788)
Tune: Thomas Campbell (1777-1844)

88 88 88 Refrain
SAGINA
www.hymnary.org/text/and_can_it_be_that_i_should_gain

# Reading 45: Psalms 127-132                    Not Fair

*If You, LORD, should keep an account of our sins and treat us
accordingly, O Lord, who could stand before you in judgment
and claim innocence?*                          Psalm 130:3-4a AMP

Life is not fair. Some people have more, some have less. Some people
are born into riches, others into poverty. Some people are smarter than
others. Some gals are prettier; some guys are more athletic. Life just isn't
fair. So why do we say life should be fair, when we know it never can be?

If we really stop to think about it, what we really mean is that we want
things to be better in our lives and the lives of those we love. Honestly,
when we complain that life isn't fair, we seldom mean that we have too
much, that we have been more blessed than others. It's usually that we
think we deserve more, we deserve better.

The cold, hard truth is this: We should be thankful that we *don't* get
what we deserve. If we only got what we deserved, Jesus never would
have suffered and died to pay the penalty for our sins. We would never
have received forgiveness, or be given second chances to come back to
Him time and time again.

What we deserve is to be left dead in our trespasses and sins
(Ephesians 2:1). What we deserve is eternal damnation (Romans 6:23).
What we deserve is to suffer the consequence of every rebellious thought,
word and deed. If life were truly fair, we would all be equally condemned,
equally miserable, equally lost, equally forever separated from God.

Let's be thankful that life isn't fair. As we come to Him today, let's
rejoice that He chose to redeem us and restore us to relationship with
Him, the Almighty Creator of heaven and earth. "For by grace you have
been saved through faith, and that not of yourselves; it is the gift of God"
(Ephesians 2:8). How truly unfair is that! Then let's fervently intercede
that He will continue to draw many others into that "unfairness", His
kingdom of Truth and Light.

# God Leads Us Along

JOHN 10:3
G. A. Y., 1903

George A. Young, 1903

1. In shad - y, green pas - tures, so rich and so sweet, God leads His dear chil-dren a - long;
2. Some - times on the mount where the sun shines so bright, God leads His dear chil-dren a - long;
3. Though sor-rows be - fall us and e - vils op-pose, God leads His dear chil-dren a - long;
4. A - way from the mire, and a - way from the clay, God leads His dear chil-dren a - long;

Where the wa-ter's cool flow bathes the wear - y one's feet, God leads His dear chil-dren a - long.
Some - times in the val - ley, in dark-est of night, God leads His dear chil-dren a - long.
Through grace we can con - quer, de - feat all our foes, God leads His dear chil-dren a - long.
A - way up in glo - ry, e - ter - ni-ty's day, God leads His dear chil-dren a - long.

*Refrain*

Some through the wa - ters, some through the flood, Some through the fire, but all through the blood;

Some through great sor - row, but God gives a song, In the night sea-son and all the day long.

# Reading 46: Psalms 133-135, 137 & 138          Preserved

*Though I walk in the midst of trouble, You preserve my life;*
*the LORD will fulfill His purpose for me...*   Psalm 138:7a-8a ESV

These verses from Psalm 138 can bring such comfort. No matter what circumstances we face in life, we can trust Him to preserve our life until His purposes have been fulfilled. Nothing and no one can interfere with His plans for us.

But sometimes we aren't exactly on board with His purposes for us. Why? Because if we had our way, we would never choose to walk "in the midst of trouble" in the first place.

That's when it helps us to remember the truth: This life is no longer about us, our comfort nor our pleasure. Now that we belong to Him, our life is all about fulfilling His purposes for us and bringing Him glory. Sometimes, "trouble" allows us to shine for Him. At other times, He uses "trouble" to prune and train us so we can mature and be more fruitful for Him.

Those of us who garden know that, left untended, a garden can quickly fill with weeds that choke out everything else. Consistent weeding, fertilizing, and pruning are necessary for a fruitful harvest.

The same is true of our human heart. Left to our own devices, we have a natural bent to sinful ways, to "weeds". We should not be surprised when "sin sprouts" pop up in our lives. A daily check-in with our Master Gardener is a great way to keep those sprouts from taking over. It certainly is less painful and less disturbing to our hearts and lives if plucked out as a little sprout than if we allow it to flourish and become a stronghold.

We will always be in need of our Master Gardener, our Redeemer and our Lord. As we read these Psalms to Him today, let's rejoice that He preserves us until His purposes are fulfilled. And as we intercede for each other and our nation, let's welcome His tender tending, so we can bear more fruit for His kingdom.

# I Must Tell Jesus

1. I must tell Jesus all of my tri-als; I can-not bear these
2. I must tell Jesus all of my trou-bles; He is a kind, com-
3. Tempt-ed and tried I need a great Sav-ior; One who can help my
4. O how the world to e-vil al-lures me! O how my heart is

bur-dens a-lone; In my dis-tress He kind-ly will help me;
pas-sion-ate Friend; If I but ask Him, He will de-liv-er,
bur-dens to bear; I must tell Je-sus, I must tell Je-sus;
tempt-ed to sin! I must tell Je-sus, and He will help me

*Chorus*

He ev-er loves and cares for His own.
Make of my trou-bles quick-ly an end.
He all my care and sor-rows will share.         I must tell Je-sus!
O-ver the world the vic-t'ry to win.

I must tell Je-sus! I can-not bear my bur-dens a-lone;

I must tell Je-sus! I must tell Je-sus! Je-sus can help me, Je-sus a-lone.

Words And Music by E. A. Hoffman

# Reading 47: Psalms 136, 139                    Trust

*You are familiar with all my ways. Before a word is on my tongue*
*    You, LORD, know it completely.*          Psalm 139:3-4 NIV

Today's focus verses are some of the strongest statements in Scripture about the intimate knowledge God has of each one of us. Can we even begin to imagine that, before we even speak a word, He already knows it *completely!* Even though it is beyond our ability to grasp or understand, that doesn't make it any less true.

This truth can help us face the unknown in our lives, particularly the uncertainty of our futures between now and the moment we are received by Jesus into heaven.

The Holocaust survivor, Corrie Ten Boom, had many moments of fear in the face of an uncertain future. In *The Hiding Place,* she shares the story of her father's response when, as a child, she tearfully told him of her fear of his death: "Father sat down on the edge of the narrow bed. 'Corrie,' he began gently, 'when you and I go to Amsterdam - when do I give you your ticket?' I sniffed a few times, considering this. 'Why, just before we get on the train.' 'Exactly. And our wise Father in heaven knows when we're going to need things, too. Don't run out ahead of Him, Corrie. When the time comes that some of us will have to die, you will look into your heart and find the strength you need - just in time.' "[25]

Corrie also shares this encouragement: "When a train goes through a tunnel and it gets dark, you don't throw away the ticket and jump off. You sit still and trust the engineer."[26]

As we read Psalms 136 and 139 to the Lord today, let's remember that our Engineer is totally trustworthy. He already knows whether or not what we fear will ever happen. If it does, He will give us the strength to face it. Nothing is a surprise to Him. He alone knows every detail of every day of our lives. He alone can be trusted with all of our moments from now until we see Him face to face.

# Leaning on the Everlasting Arms

Text: Elisha A. Hoffman (1839-1929)
Tune: Anthony J. Showalter (1858-1924)

10 9 10 9 Refrain
SHOWALTER
www.hymnary.org/text/what_a_fellowship_what_a_joy_divine

# Reading 48: Psalms 140-143          The Joy of Surrender

*Show me the way I should go, for to You I entrust my life.*
                                                    Psalm 143:8 NIV

Reading Psalms 140 through 143, it's impossible not to feel David's anger and fear. He is being hunted down just because he stepped out in faith, slew a giant, and became an overnight sensation.

As He cries out to God, his words reflect his anxiety. But, after all his pleading for God to change his circumstances - as well as rain down destruction on his enemies - he says "Show me the way I should go, for to You I entrust my life" (Psalm 143:8 NIV). He has finally come to that joyous point of surrender.

Joy in surrender? Isn't surrender just a sign of weakness and admission of failure? How could there possibly be joy in surrender?

Joy actually can most often *only* be found on the other side of surrender. Let's consider that thought for a moment.

Proverbs 3:5 says we should trust Him whole-heartedly instead of our own understanding, our own way of doing things. Here's an example: Jesus tells us to love our enemies and pray for those who persecute us (Matthew 5:44). That makes no sense to us. "They don't deserve it!" They don't. But when we surrender to His way, we find hatred, bitterness and anger can be washed away with a flood of peace and joy.

His way gives us a different perspective. As we release our enemies to Him, we remember this life is just temporary. He may have a greater purpose in this situation than we could ever see with our own eyes. Choosing to do it His way allows us to find rest, joy and peace in Him, our sovereign Redeemer and Lord.

As we read through David's complaints and pleas today, let us follow his example and, in the end, lift up our soul to Him in prayer, surrendering all to His way and His will. With Jesus, may we pray "Your will be done" (Matthew 26:42), and then rest in the joy of surrender to Him and His ways.

# Be Still My Soul

Words by Katharina von Schlegel, Tr. by Jane L. Borthwick
Music by Jean Sibelius

# Reading 49: Psalms 144-146                    Wait

*The Lord is gracious and full of compassion,*
*slow to anger and great in mercy.*     Psalm 145:8

Because our God is gracious, compassionate, slow to anger and rich in mercy, He is patient. As we look back, we can see how He has been so patient with us as we struggled to come to, and stay in, dependence on Him. Yet, we often fight impatience when we don't see immediate answers to our prayers.

If we believe we are trusting Him, then why do we fight impatience? Is it because we don't *really* trust Him to accomplish it in *His* time, in *His* way, and in *His* plan? Are we thinking "God, I have such a good plan. It's in keeping with Your will. Why aren't You doing my plan as I have asked it to be done?"

Though we don't realize it, what we may be saying is "My will be done." Take our prayers for the return of our prodigals, for example. It's a good will. We want what He wants. And it is for the eternal benefit of those we love. However, we are frustrated when we don't see the answer – now already.

We say we trust Him to accomplish it in His time. But in the meantime, we are anxious and worried. Maybe part of what we want is for God to answer our prayer so we feel that we don't need to worry anymore. As if our worrying can accomplish anything. No, Jesus spends 10 verses in Matthew 6:25-34 telling us not to worry about anything!

As we read our Psalms to Him and intercede once more, let's make sure we have handed all our anxieties over, *totally* handed them over, to His perfect plan. Let's confirm with Him that we have truly let go so He is free to do His work. Then let's look ahead to the future without worry, and spend time thanking Him now for the way in which He is answering our prayers. He *is* working out all the details in our lives. Though the way may be thorny, there will be a joyful end.

# Blessed Assurance, Jesus Is Mine

Text: Fanny J. Crosby, 1820-1915
Tune: Phoebe Palmer Knapp, 1839-1908

Irregular
ASSURANCE
www.hymnary.org/text/blessed_assurance_jesus_is_mine

# Reading 50: Psalms 147-150      Facing the Future

*He counts the number of the stars; He calls them all by name.*

Psalm 147:4

We can tell ourselves that we are not afraid of the future. We can recite verse after verse telling us not to fear. We can remind ourselves that, regardless of what the future holds, our eternal destiny is secure. And yet, fear of the future can loom large when we see God allow a difficulty, sadness, or loss in someone else's life. What if God calls us to suffer similar challenges, trials, or tests? And fear can begin.

We tell ourselves that we just want to be ready in case the worst should happen. But what we are really trying to do is be God. We want to see into our future. Ultimately, what we are doing is entertaining the great deceiver, whose fearful whisperings are intended not to warn and prepare, but instead to kill, steal, and destroy.

Our enemy wants to kill our dependence and our trust in God. He wants to steal our peace and our joy. He wants to destroy our witness by moving our focus from the God of Peace to the fear of potential circumstances.

How many times have we anticipated grief or braced for the worst, only to have it not happen? How much joy and peace have we forfeited? How productive for him, our enemy, but how counter-productive for us.

As we lift today's Psalms of praise to our Almighty God, let's remind ourselves that He counts the stars; He alone calls them all by name. Let's rejoice that He already knows all our future, every single moment He has planned for each one of us until He welcomes us home. There is no place for fear.

In intercession, let's stand firm in our faith, with our armor in place. Let's raise our shield of faith, quench that fiery dart of fear and send it back to the pit of hell where it came from. Then let's boldly march forward and reclaim surrendered territory, remembering it is all about Him, His purposes, His kingdom and His glory.

# GOING FORWARD

*For I am not ashamed of the Gospel of Christ, for it is the power of God to salvation for everyone who believes.*

Romans 1:16

## What's Next?

We have been faithful to answer His call to "stand in the gap" on behalf of our nation.

We have completed the 31 Days of Preparation prior to battle. We prayed and fasted on New Year's Day as the Lord led. We stood firm, engaged the enemy, and brought praises, prayers and petitions to the Throne of Grace for 50 days. Now what?

Hopefully, we have been drawn closer to our Lord though this process, are walking with a renewed spirit and refreshed heart now more full of faith, and are encouraged in the truth that prayer changes things.

As we move forward, let's ask the Lord to show us precisely how He wants to continue to bring change not only to our individual lives, but to the lives of our families, our businesses, our churches, our schools, our communities and to all levels of leadership in our nation.

Let us truly become His people again, a people who reflect and resemble our gracious and forgiving Heavenly Father. Let's offer the Lord our bodies as cleansed and useful vessels for His blessing, using our resources to be the hands and feet of Jesus in our needy world. Let's be a passionate people who are not just talking about, but actually living out the "good news", as a testimony that speaks not only to our next-door neighbor, but reaches around the globe, impacting generations to come.

Let's continue to keep our swords sharpened by committing to stay in the Word, choosing to follow its wisdom and direction as our moral compass instead of leaning on our own understanding. Let's continue using our powerful weapon of prayer to bring about the changes He desires, both in our hearts as well as the hearts and lives of those we love.

As His eyes continue to search "to and fro throughout the whole earth" (II Chronicles 16:9) looking to support those whose hearts are fully devoted to Him, may He see us, faithfully continuing to "stand in the gap." May we continue to ask Him for renewal of our hearts, restoration of His place on the throne of our lives, and revival in our land.

If we will...then He will.

*For God so loved the world that He gave His only begotten Son, that whoever believes in Him should not perish but have everlasting life. For God did not send His Son into the world to condemn the world, but that the world through Him might be saved.*

*He who believes in Him is not condemned; but he who does not believe is condemned already, because he has not believed in the name of the only begotten Son of God.*

John 3:16-18

# BIBLIOGRAPHY

## How Did We Get Here?? – page 4
[1] George Washington's 1789 Thanksgiving Proclamation - www.mountvernon.org/education/primary-sources-2/article/thanksgiving-proclamation-of-1789/

## The Power of Prayer – pages 9-11
[2] www.historyonthenet.com/when-patton-enlisted-the-entire-third-army-to-pray-for-fair-weather

[3] Msgr. James H. O'Neill, "The True Story of the Patton Prayer", 1950, (From the Review of the News, 6 October 1971)

[4] Ibid.

[5] Ibid.

[6] Ibid.

[7] Public domain – published and distributed by the United States Army, 1944

## December 14 – page 43
[8] Christ-Centered Mall, www.christcenteredmall.com/teachings/armor-of-god-2.htm

## December 15 – page 45
[9] Dave Johnson, "What is the Breastplate of Righteousness?", www.lifehopeandtruth.com/change/christian-conversion/armor-of-god/breastplate-of-righteousness/

[10] www.gotquestions.org/breastplate-of-righteousness.html

## December 31 – page 77
[11] Priscilla Shirer, "A Life in Alignment", Passion Conference 2018, January 5, 2018

[12] Walt Disney Pictures, *The Lion King*, 1994

## New Year's Day – Call to Prayer and Fasting – page 79
[13] Wayne Grudem, *Systematic Theology: An Introduction to Biblical Doctrine* (Grand Rapids: Zondervan, 1994, 2000), p. 391

## Reading 20 – page 129

[14] https://buffalonews.com/news/ogrady-recounts-survival-rescue-f-16-fighter-pilot-sobs-as-tape-of-first-radio-contact/article_4934e5f0-0034-5c04-a9d9-455a

## Reading 24 – page 137

[15] https://spacemath.gsfc.nasa.gov › weekly

[16] Louie Giglio, *How Great Is Our God: 100 Indescribable Devotions about God and Science*, (Nashville: Tommy Nelson, 2019) pp. 36-37

## Reading 26 – page 141

[17] decisionmagazine.com/abortion-the-leading-cause-of-death-in-2021/, quoting statistics from Worldometer.com and the World Health Organization.

[18] Ibid.

[19] Ibid.

## Reading 34 – page 157

[20] Martin Luther, as quoted by Charles R. Swindoll, *THE HYMNAL for Worship & Celebration*, (Waco: Word Music, 1986) Foreword

[21] Ibid.

## Reading 38 – page 165

[22] Josephus, *Contra Apionem* I.37–44, as cited in Dunkelgrün, T. The *Testimonium Flavianum Canonicum*: Josephus as a Witness to the Biblical Canon, 1566–1823. *Int class trad* **23**, 252–268 (2016). https://doi.org/10.1007/s12138-016-0408-4

[23] James MacDonald, *God Wrote a Book*, (Wheaton: Crossway, 2002, 2004), p. 18

## Reading 42 – page 173

[24] Scott Hubbard, https://www.desiringgod.org/articles/better-to-have-a-burden, 09/12/2022

## Reading 47 – page 183

[25] Corrie Ten Boom, *The Hiding Place*, (New York: Crossings Classics, 1971, 1984), p. 27
[26]

[26] Corrie Ten Boom Quotes. BrainyQuote.com, BrainyMedia Inc, 2022. https://www.brainyquote.com/quotes/corrie_ten_boom_393675

Dear Reader,

Thank you for sharing our heart for revival in this nation. We pray that you have been blessed and encouraged by this prayer project.

It has been a joy to connect with so many of you through our Facebook page (Facebook.com/ifwewillthenhewill) as well as through our website (www.ifwewill.com). Your excitement and faithfulness have continued to confirm our call. In turn, may you be encouraged by the fact that this is one of many "brush fires" the Lord has ignited for revival in hearts all across this nation. Our Almighty God is on the move!

If you have any questions about this prayer project or would like more information, you can leave a comment on our website or email us directly at dawn@ifwewill.com.

A free and complete copy of this manuscript is available on our website for downloading and/or printing in case you have friends who cannot afford to purchase a book or who may prefer larger print.

Lastly, book reviews are one of the most effective methods to encourage others to join in this battle. If you would take a moment to rate this project and write a brief review on the website of the business where you purchased this book, we would greatly appreciate it.

Thank you again for standing in the gap with us on behalf of our nation and our world. May you be blessed as you joyfully give yourself to Him for His purposes, for His glory and His kingdom.

A Three Strand Cord (Ecclesiastes 4:12)

Made in the USA
Columbia, SC
15 November 2024

46616582R00115